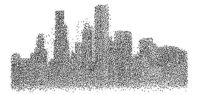

RESURRECTING HOPE

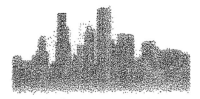

RESURRECTING HOPE

John M. Perkins
with Jo Kadlecek

Regal Books
A Division of Gospel Light
Ventura, California, U.S.A.

Published by Regal Books
A Division of Gospel Light
Ventura, California, U.S.A.

Regal Books is a ministry of Gospel Light, an evangelical Christian publisher dedicated to serving the local church. We believe God's vision for Gospel Light is to provide church leaders with
biblical, user-friendly materials that will help them evangelize, disciple and minister to children,
youth and families.

It is our prayer that this Regal Book will help you discover biblical truth for your own life and
help you meet the needs of others. May God richly bless you.

For a free catalog of resources from Regal Books/Gospel Light please contact your Christian supplier or call
1-800-4-GOSPEL.

Library of Congress Cataloging-in-Publication Data
Perkins, John, 1930-
    Resurrecting hope / John M. Perkins with Jo Kadlecek.
    p. cm.
    ISBN 0-8307-1810-9 (trade)
    1. City missions. 2. City churches. I. Kadlecek, Jo.
II. Title.
BV2653.P47 1995   95-8990
250'.973—dc20   CIP

1 2 3 4 5 6 7 8 9 10 11 12 13 14 15 / 02 01 00 99 98 97 96 95

Rights for publishing this book in other languages are contracted by Gospel Literature International
(GLINT). GLINT also provides technical help for the adaptation, translation and publishing of Bible
study resources and books in scores of languages worldwide. For further information, contact
GLINT, P.O. Box 4060, Ontario, CA 91761-1003, U.S.A., or the publisher.

CONTENTS

◨

Acknowledgments   7

Introduction: Good in the 'Hood   11

1. Upon This Rock   17

Reconciliation

2. Back to the Future   27
   Voice of Calvary Fellowship and
   Mendenhall Bible Church in Mississippi

3. Of Partners and Process   39
   The Chapel and Arlington Road Church of God in Akron, Ohio

4. A United *Christian* Nations   51
   First Baptist Church of Flushing in Queens, New York

Relocation

5. Daddy, Are You Going to Be a Sermon Today?   67
   Lawndale Community Church in Chicago, Illinois

6. Holy Ground   81
   Church in the City in Denver, Colorado

7. The Real Graceland   95
   Mississippi Boulevard Christian Church in Memphis, Tennessee

8. Building Hope on Sand   107
   New Song Community Church in Baltimore, Maryland

Redistribution

9. The Church Next Door   123
   Lake Avenue Congregational Church in Pasadena, California

10. From Riots to Renaissance   135
    West Angeles Church of God in Christ in Los Angeles, California

11. Manhattan Transformation   147
    Redeemer Presbyterian Church in Manhattan, New York

Conclusion

12. There *Is* a Balm   161

Acknowledgments

We would like humbly to thank the many, many people who helped make this book possible. We deeply appreciate the following friends taking time out from their demanding schedules (urban ministers are busy people!) to talk with us, share their visions with us and show us their work:

Pastors Artis and Carolyn Fletcher and Dolphus and Rosie Weary from Mendenhall Bible Church and the Mendenhall Ministries; Pastors Phil and Marcia Reed, Spencer and Nancy Perkins, Chris and Donna Rice at Voice of Calvary Fellowship; Melvin and Thelma Anderson at Voice of Calvary Ministries, the Antioch Community and the *Urban Family* magazine staff—all in Mississippi.

Copastors Wayne and Anne Gordon and Carey and Melanie Casey, and Precious Thomas at Lawndale Community Church in Chicago, Illinois.

Copastors Russ Rosser, Jorge Prado and Henry Kwan; lay leader Iris Holder and the amazing staff at First Baptist Church of Flushing in Queens, New York.

Senior Pastor Alvin Jackson and his wife, Tina, Vera Banks, Andre Williams, Jackie McHenry and the friendly staff at Mississippi Boulevard Christian Church in Memphis, Tennessee.

Pastor Gordon Kirks, Roger Bosch, Steve Klein, Priscilla Perkins and my church family at Lake Avenue Congregational Church in Pasadena, California.

Ralph and Bonnie Gatti for their insights and hospitality, Bob Sturkey, Pastor Knute Larson at The Chapel and Doctors Ronald Fowler and Diana Swoops at Arlington Road Church of God in Akron, Ohio.

Pastors Michael and Brenda Walker and Jude and Cindy Del

Hierra, Barbara Thompson, Ade Ajaila, Alice Rafuse, Jimmy Pritchett, Linden Morris and the College and Career Sunday School members (our next leaders) at Church in the City in Denver, Colorado.

Pastor Mark Gornik, Allan and Susan Tibbels, Torey Reynolds, LaVerne Cooper, Clyde Harris, Steve Smallman, Wy Plummer and the Christian family at New Song Community Church in Baltimore, Maryland.

Pastor Tim and Kathy Keller, Yvonne Dodd, Jeff White, Janet Grams and Patrick Burke at Redeemer Presbyterian Church in Manhattan, New York.

Bishop Charles and Mae Blake, Kenneth Hammonds, Frank Robinson, Lula Bailey and the gracious staff at West Angeles Church of God in Christ in Los Angeles, California.

And, of course, our editor, Kyle Duncan, at Regal Books/Gospel Light, without whom we could not have proceeded with this project.

We warmly dedicate this book to all the people who are a part of the Christian Community Development Association (CCDA) movement. We are grateful for their untiring Christian example in serving our communities. Specifically, we dedicate this book to the following CCDA servant-leaders who serve on the board of directors:

Rev. Wayne Gordon, Lawndale Community Church, Chicago, Illinois, *President;*

Rev. Noel Castellanos, La Villita Community Church, Chicago, Illinois, *Vice Chairman;*

Mr. Ted Travis, Neighborhood Ministries, Denver, Colorado, *Secretary;*

Dr. Robert Sturkey, Akron, Ohio, *Treasurer;*

Ms. Edith Davis, Spring Arbor College, Jackson, Mississippi;

Mr. Harvey Drake Jr., Emerald City Outreach Ministries, Seattle, Washington;

Ms. Donna Holt, Bellville, Illinois;

Mr. Glen Kehrein, Circle Urban Ministries, Chicago, Illinois;

Dr. Robert Lupton, FCS Urban Ministries, Atlanta, Georgia;

Mr. Steve Morris, World Impact, Fresno, California;

Rev. Herman Moten, Christian Resource Center, Tampa, Florida;

Dr. Mary Nelson, Bethel New Life, Chicago, Illinois;

Rev. Elizar Pagan, Discipleship Chapel, Inc., Brooklyn, New York;

Mr. Spencer Perkins, *Urban Family* magazine, Jackson, Mississippi;
Mr. H. Spees, Youth for Christ, Fresno, California;
Mr. Robert Woolfolk, Community Outreach Service Center, Denver, Colorado.

CCDA Advisory Board

Rev. Dolphus Weary, Mendenhall Ministries, Mendenhall, Mississippi;
Dr. Keith Phillips, World Impact, Inc., Los Angeles, California;
Rev. Haman Cross Jr., Rosedale Park Baptist Church, Detroit, Michigan;
Ms. Kathy Dudley, Voice of Hope Ministries, Dallas, Texas;
Dr. Vera Mae Perkins, Foundation for Reconciliation and Development, Pasadena, California;
Rev. Ron Spann, Church of the Messiah, Detroit, Michigan;
Dr. Ray Bakke, International Urban Association, Chicago, Illinois;
Dr. Ron Sider, Eastern College, St. Davids, Pennsylvania;
Mr. Howard Ahmanson, Field Company, Newport Beach, California.

Introduction: Good in the 'Hood

■

This book is about good news. It is a book of stories, all true, about courageous contemporary Christians who, through their local churches, are making a powerful difference in their urban neighborhoods. It is a book about black, Hispanic and white partnerships from churches in the inner cities, suburbs and rural communities working together to proclaim the gospel of Jesus Christ. It is about congregations of Christians willing to love their neighbors so much that they are also willing to take responsibility for the economic, educational and spiritual welfare of the families in their neighborhoods.

Hope, Redemption and Change

This is a book about hope, redemption and change—qualities not often associated with the inner city, but qualities that are as real there as the concrete playgrounds and housing projects found in every American inner city.

In 1993, we celebrated our fifth annual conference for our national organization, the Christian Community Development Association (CCDA), by returning home to Jackson, Mississippi. CCDA is a growing national network of people, urban ministries and churches committed to working together to restore and redeem our communities for Christ through holistic ministry. Pastor Noel Castellanos of La Villita Community Church in Chicago, Illinois, served as our emcee in Jackson, enthusiastically challenging the one thousand attending members by asking a question I've not been able to forget since. His question was not unlike the disciples' question when they asked, "Can anything good come out of Nazareth?" (John 1:46, *NKJV*). Pastor

Castellanos repeatedly asked us, "Can anything good come from the 'hood?" We all know the answer was, and is, an emphatic yes, in spite of what the media tries to tell us. So with great joy, this book is an attempt to show you that a whole lot of good is, in fact, coming from the 'hood.

From Mendenhall, Mississippi, to New York City, New York, to Los Angeles, California, good news is being preached on the street corners of busy and diverse communities in a variety of creative ministries. As I have traveled across the country, I have seen that in virtually every city, evangelical, Bible-believing churches are making a positive impact in their cities for Christ. They represent a growing concern, actively expressed by Christians for their urban neighbors— Christians who are committed to the principles of Christian community development. More exciting still, they come from all denominations, cultures and backgrounds, but they are driven by one purpose: to demonstrate God's love to their communities.

Pockets of Hope

And so in this book, we tell the stories of urban congregations—what I call America's "pockets of hope"—proving to the world that there is a balm in Gilead, a healing force that is changing our inner cities forever. These are stories from churches such as Mississippi Boulevard Christian Church in Memphis, Tennessee; Church in the City in Denver, Colorado; First Baptist Church of Flushing, New York; Lawndale Community Church in Chicago, Illinois; West Angeles Church of God in Christ in Los Angeles, California; Redeemer Presbyterian Church in Manhattan, New York.

These also include churches such as The Chapel and Arlington Road Church of God in Akron, Ohio; New Song Community Church in Baltimore, Maryland; Lake Avenue Congregational Church in Pasadena, California; Voice of Calvary and Mendenhall Bible Church in Mississippi. Each of these churches represents a bigger army of God's people that are confronting three hundred years of racial tension and social oppression through loving, creative and intentional efforts.

Of course, Church in the City, First Baptist, Mendenhall Bible Church and the others profiled in this book are not the only churches in the United States having a positive influence on their communities. I thank God that hundreds of other churches are sending missionaries to the nations as well as to the ghettos, discipling new believers in the faith, mentoring their youth and challenging their families to pray together.

The churches described here are simply a few examples of the many congregations who have begun responding to the complex problems of our inner cities by providing positive, practical solutions. They are solid evidence that the evangelical church can have a wonderful influence on urban America. By placing values on the principles of Christian community development—that is, reconciliation, relocation and redistribution—these churches are winning their neighbors to Jesus. In story after story, their exciting work and untiring devotion communicates the powerful truth of the good news of God's redemptive love. And in a variety of ways, they are proclaiming the simple fact: Much good can come from the 'hood.

Helping Their Neighbors

I believe the stories of these churches are similar to another incident I learned of not long ago. Two young black men recently were walking through their inner-city community to the corner store for sodas. For years, Junior, a handsome, muscular 19-year-old with a winsome smile, had known his buddy Ricardo, a slender peer of the same age. They had grown up together in this same neighborhood. Although neither man graduated from high school, both men knew the meaning of hard work and were proud of their construction jobs. As they passed alleys, historic houses and laughing children, they talked of friends, bosses and the weather. But all of a sudden, an unimaginable event interrupted their conversation and diverted their attention.

"Hey, look at that!" Junior was pointing to a dilapidated house they had passed a hundred times before on regular trips to the store. They had often spoken with the elderly woman who lived alone in the two-story, 50-year-old house. She would ask them about their mothers and they would ask about her children. Sometimes, the three would sit together on her front porch as the tiny gray-haired woman shared stories, cookies and grandmotherly advice with her young friends. In return, they would pick up eggs and sugar from the store for her.

This particular afternoon, though, as they passed the huge old home, they saw that the side wall was literally beginning to crumble. Drain pipes and shingles were starting to drop from the roof. Glass started to pop out from the upstairs bedrooms. Through the shattering window below, the two friends could see the older woman talking in the kitchen on the telephone, completely unaware of the danger she was about to face.

"Miss Maudie, get out of there fast!" The men screamed to her through the window, but she couldn't hear them. Worried that their elderly friend was about to be buried alive, Junior and Ricardo raced through the front door, grabbed Miss Maudie and escorted her safely away from the crumbling house. As soon as the three settled across the street, they turned back toward the house just in time to watch the entire wall collapse into a pile of drywall, beams and broken glass.

Within minutes, the block was teeming with police cars, fire trucks, curious neighbors and television reporters. A host of officials questioned the three friends about the destruction of Miss Maudie's house. Together, Junior and Ricardo told officers and reporters how they had been walking to the store, noticed the wall starting to fall, yelled to Miss Maudie to get out, and when she hadn't heard them, they ran inside to pull her to safety.

"They saved my life, these boys did," the gray-haired woman told the crowd. Ricardo and Junior were reluctant heroes, claiming that they were just doing what anyone else would do: helping their neighbor. As police reports were filed, television stories made and neighbors returned to their homes, the two young men finally made their way to the store. The event had made them more thirsty than ever.

Though no mention of Ricardo and Junior's efforts made the evening news that night, the two young men had indeed saved the life of their elderly neighbor. Undoubtedly, television and newspaper journalists in their city missed a special opportunity to paint an accurate picture of life in urban America, the truth that much good is happening in the 'hood. Certainly, many problems demand our attention and concern, and they will ultimately require the whole Body of Christ in America to work together to resolve. But I thank God that Junior and Ricardo represent a wonderful army of modern-day good Samaritans who are willing to enter potentially dangerous situations to lay down their lives for their neighbors.

Without question, the response from these young men to the tragedy they witnessed—that they were just "helping their neighbor"—must become our own. Thankfully, many congregations of "neighbors" across the country have begun to respond to what are often crumbling situations in our poor neighborhoods. Their courageous efforts are reminders to us all that if we fail to enter the opportunities and challenges that encompass our inner cities, the very future of our nation is threatened.

Good News

As a veteran urban worker and Christian community developer, I am both grateful for and proud of the churches represented in this book. Their stories are gospel proof of the good being done in inner cities throughout the United States. My hope is that their examples might help communicate the transforming power of the gospel, which as I've said for years, is the visible demonstration of God's love. Their innovative, courageous and practical efforts in ministry provide helpful insights for those pastors, church members and other leaders who are equally concerned for our urban neighbors. From them, I believe we can gain a clearer perspective of our own roles and strategies as, together, we win the lost in our communities.

Of course, we all know that much work remains to be done for all Christians if we are going to save our cities for Christ. But these 12 churches give us hope and inspiration so that when we work across denominational, cultural and economic lines, we can win some of the battles we see on every street corner in urban America. In the process, it is my prayer that we will see a clearer picture of God's heart for reconciliation, restoration and unity as the Kingdom of heaven is advanced on earth.

The special and individual stories of these churches on the following pages are good news indeed. And in this day and age, we could all use a little more of that.

Upon This Rock

Looking Back

When I was six years old, I went to school for the first time in my small segregated hometown in Mississippi. I was excited to be in a classroom. As a little boy, I somehow believed that everything about school would play an important role in my development. In those days, teachers were allowed to use the Bible for instruction, so my teacher taught my classmates and me the Lord's Prayer: "Our Father who art in heaven, hallowed be Thy name. Thy Kingdom come. Thy will be done, on earth as it is in heaven" (Matt. 6:9,10, *NASB*).

As we would repeat the prayer in class, I started to believe that heaven on earth was a key aspect of the gospel. In fact, that became a point of reference for me in my understanding of the Christian faith. You see, most of my people believed that though their lives were unjust, when they got to heaven, there would finally be justice.

I was confused, then, when the same white folks who were known as good, church-going citizens throughout town would come to our house to buy the whiskey my relatives would illegally sell. These religious white folks would get their liquor, talk disrespectfully to my elders and then go on their way as if nothing was wrong with their actions. Not only that, but local black churchgoers would come and buy whiskey as well. The same folks were at their churches each Sunday, serving as ushers, deacons or Sunday School teachers. You can understand why I grew up feeling suspicious of the Church. As a young child, I didn't see much of heaven on earth in the lives of these religious people.

When I was a teenager, my older brother was killed by white police officers and I left Mississippi to come to California. I was concerned entirely with my own economic status, forgot about religion and believed California offered opportunities for me to earn money that I would never find back home. My attitude toward church was similar to my business ethic: Church people were just good people who worked hard for themselves. Christianity to me was just like joining a country club to be with people who were like you. Imagine my surprise when I began experiencing something different. In California, I saw for the first time in my life white and black Christians working toward racial reconciliation.

After I became a Christian through my son's involvement in Child Evangelism Fellowship, some godly white men chose to disciple me. I began to see in them a different brand of Christianity from what I had seen in Mississippi. Through intense Bible study and prayer times together, they were modeling to me the kingdom of God on earth. It became clear to me that the gospel was good news for all people of all economic situations and races. From these men, I learned that Jesus Christ lived, died and rose again so we would know the transforming love of God. The gospel was to be the demonstration of that love on earth. Eventually, it also became clear that I was to take that message back to Mississippi, and I had the faithful prayers and support of my white brothers in California.

Going Home

When I returned to Mississippi, I knew I was called to minister to my people and to teach the Bible to them. White folks in the South were saying the same thing I was, but I quickly saw that no relationship existed between their talk as far as relating the gospel message to us was concerned and the poverty in which their neighbors lived.

I believed that the white church had married its religious values to the American culture of materialism and segregation, so the concept of reconciliation was foreign to them. The poverty and economic injustice was incredible (railroad tracks literally divided our town). Relationships between white and black Christians were greatly lacking. And those people wanting to pursue reconciliation were often discouraged by their denominations.

Then two local white pastors who had tried to reach out to us began to feel a pressure they thought was too great to endure. Within months of each other, these two Christian men committed suicide and I knew at that point that something was really wrong in Mississippi. The nonviolent Civil Rights Movement led by Dr. Martin Luther King Jr. was becoming clearer and stronger, and we joined that cause with a vengeance. It became the focus of our ministry. I don't think I realized then that a supportive environment for white people to change was almost nonexistent. We simply knew that racism was the law of the land and we were determined to change that.

The problem was, as I was to find out, that too often we ended up fighting white people with the Civil Rights Movement. We were so busy trying to get freedom, and the white folks were so cruel in their reaction to the movement, that it kept us from experiencing any true biblically based reconciliation. White folks thought if we got "saved enough" we would give up our fight for civil rights. But my vision for coming home was to share the gospel with my people, not with white people.

I realized white folks were locked into their culture while my concern was for winning black folks to Jesus and improving their economic situations. I had not formed any mission for white people, unless they would come and join us in our civil rights efforts, or if they would help our people in practical ways, such as teaching them to read better. I didn't really believe reconciliation could happen so I didn't share the gospel with white people because I didn't think I had come home for them. I was blind to my responsibility to stress evangelism regardless of race.

Learning to Love

Then, without warning, I landed in jail in the nearby town of Brandon for leading a civil rights protest. While there, I began to understand the depths of the depravity of racism. I was beaten by police officers almost to the point of death. Amazingly, though, as my blood was splattered on the floor and my stomach kicked by the white officers who were "teaching the nigger a lesson," I also realized the depths of God's powerful love. I saw clearly that the gospel message of unity had to be a priority.

I made a bargain with God: If He got me out of this place alive, I would begin to preach a gospel I knew was stronger than my race, my economic interests and my culture. I would preach a gospel that could reconcile black and white, Jew and Gentile together in one Body. God obviously spared my life and got me out of jail. He also held me to my end of the bargain. Thankfully, He didn't let me off the hook.

Perhaps God used an early experience in my life to show me the power of love, a love that would enable me to endure that jail beating. I have a vivid picture in my mind of the first time in my life I can remember being with my earthly father. My mother died when I was seven months old and so my father gave us to my grandmother, though he stayed with us my first year. He then went away looking for work. I didn't see him again until I was four years old, and he had come by to visit us. I remember clearly how he embraced me, accepted me and told me he loved me. From that point on, I knew how powerful a father's love for his son could be.

So when I accepted Jesus Christ as my personal Savior, the great truths of the gospel were ignited into my life: love, acceptance and forgiveness. But my Brandon jail experience taught me that I hadn't understood the whole purpose of the gospel: Our heavenly Father loved us so much that He sent His only Son to be crucified for our sakes so we would be reconciled to Him and to each other.

After the Brandon jail experience, I began to change the way I thought. I saw that to be a Christian meant to be an ongoing demonstration of the gospel. That meant no justifiable separation of race or class could be present in the Body. It meant that I could no longer write someone off as a racist because that would be saying he was unredeemable or not worthy of God's love. And it meant that for the first time in my life I had to consider that this same gospel that had changed me could change white people, not just give them a patronizing excuse to help me help other blacks.

The Three Rs of Christian Community Development

Relocation

At that point, I believe God also began to show me the three basic principles of Christian community development, principles I believe Christians must adhere to as God builds His Church. The first is what I call "relocation," or living among the poor. It means desiring for your neighbor and your neighbor's family what you desire for yourself and your family. Living the gospel means bettering the quality of other people's lives—spiritually, physically, socially and emotionally—as you better your own. Living the gospel means sharing in the suffering and pain of others.

How did Jesus love? "The Word became flesh, and dwelt among us, and we beheld His glory, glory as of the only begotten from the

Father, full of grace and truth" (John 1:14, *NASB*). Jesus relocated. He became one of us. He didn't commute back and forth to heaven. Similarly, I began to see that the most effective messenger of the gospel to the poor would also live among the poor to whom God called him.

By relocating, we will understand most clearly the real problems facing the poor; then we may begin to look for real solutions to change our communities. For example, if our children are a part of that community, you can be certain we will do whatever we can to ensure that

JESUS SAID THAT THE ESSENCE OF

CHRISTIANITY COULD BE SUMMED UP IN TWO

INSEPARABLE COMMANDMENTS: LOVE GOD

AND LOVE YOUR NEIGHBORS.

the children of our community get a good education. Relocation transforms "you, them and theirs" to "we, us and ours." Effective ministries plant and build communities of believers that have a personal stake in developing their neighborhoods.

Reconciliation

The second key principle in Christian community development is reconciliation; spiritual, cultural and economic reconciliation must occur if holistic ministry is to be achieved. Coming home to Mississippi taught me that reconciliation is at the heart of the gospel. Jesus said that the essence of Christianity could be summed up in two inseparable commandments: Love God and love your neighbors.

Too often we presume that the power of the gospel will reconcile people to God and to each other, but we don't follow through on that reality or plan to make it happen. To fulfill the ministry of reconciliation (according to 2 Cor. 5) we have to become intentional. We begin by first confessing that we are all brothers and sisters and then by seeking to reach those people who are different from us. Christian community development is concerned with reconciling people to God and with bringing them into a church fellowship where they can be discipled in their faith.

But can a gospel that reconciles people to God without reconciling people to others be the true gospel of Jesus Christ? Our love for Christ should break down every racial, ethnic and economic barrier. As Christians come together to solve the problems of their communities, the great challenge will be to partner and witness together across these barriers. The task of loving the poor is shared by the entire Body of Christ—black, white, brown and yellow, rich and poor, urban and suburban.

So we must abandon the twentieth-century marketing strategy incorporated by evangelicalism that church growth can only happen in

WHEN THE BODY OF CHRIST IS VISIBLY PRESENT AND LIVING AMONG THE POOR (*RELOCATION*), AND WHEN WE ARE LOVING OUR NEIGHBORS AND OUR NEIGHBORS' FAMILIES THE WAY WE LOVE OURSELVES AND OUR OWN FAMILIES (*RECONCILIATION*), THE RESULT IS *REDISTRIBUTION*.

homogeneous settings. We are not called to make disciples just for the sake of numbers. We are to make disciples who understand the reconciling aspect of the gospel and who can go into all the world. True disciples are to help in the healing of others now, healing the racism, prejudices and hurt by reflecting God's kingdom on earth.

Redistribution

Once this healing occurs, believers can address the issues of social action and economic development by ministering to the felt needs of their communities. This is the third principle of Christian community development called "redistribution." When the Body of Christ is visibly present and living among the poor (*relocation*), and when we are loving our neighbors and our neighbors' families the way we love ourselves and our own families (*reconciliation*), the result is *redistribution*.

If we as God's people, along with our resources, are living in or close to a poor community and are a part of it, our skills and our resources will be applied to the problems of that community. Bringing our lives, our skills, our education and our resources and putting them to work to empower people in a community of need is redistribution. Christian community development ministries and churches find creative avenues to create jobs, schools, health centers, home ownership and other enterprises of long-term development. This book is full of exciting examples of such ministries committed to the three Rs.

Setting the Stage

When the three Rs exist, we implement what I call the felt-need concept. Humans have three fundamental needs: the need to be loved, the need for significance and the need for a reasonable amount of security. Meeting these needs, then, affirms the dignity of all people. The three Rs must be anchored in the felt-need concept. When this happens, the Church displays the true love of God and the poor are empowered.

When Jesus intentionally went through Samaria—what some today might call "the bad part of town"—He stopped on His journey at a well. Scripture tells us in John 4 that while there, Jesus met a Samaritan woman, a woman regarded by many as shady at best. Recognizing they were at the well for the same reason, Jesus responded to her felt need and then went a step beyond: He became water for her. He met her at her deepest need, setting an example for all Christians as they minister His love to the felt needs of our neighbors.

This is the stage from which we proclaim the stories of contemporary churches that are working toward Christian community development. God has entrusted a sense of the whole gospel into their hands, and into our hands. As a result, He has brought about a movement known as the Christian Community Development Association (CCDA). CCDA is a grassroots movement of humble Christian servants more concerned about changing their communities than about challenging their local political representatives on the nightly news.

The following chapters present wonderful stories of contemporary churches that represent the collective backdrop of such a struggle to win back our communities for Christ. These churches have that vision and are passing it on. They show us what it means to walk upright with God in humility. Most of these churches are members of CCDA, which is a national network of churches, individuals and ministries committed to these principles. I believe CCDA and the stories of these churches are treasures of hope for our whole nation and land. These churches understand that good news must be given away; it doesn't belong to us. What any of us have we must realize is not our own.

Yet, just understanding these principles is not enough. Walking in humility as a servant is what God blesses. He resists the proud and gives grace to the humble. A conversion needs to occur in the Church to address the many problems of our communities. And our country is ready for it.

President Bill Clinton ran for the presidency on "ending welfare as we know it." But no one in Washington seems to agree on how government can accomplish that. I believe the alternatives to welfare and other social problems are clear and the churches profiled in this book prove that. They represent a powerful army of God's people working together to solve the problems of our cities—problems the government can never solve alone.

From coast to coast, city to city, God is building His Church, and consequently, that Church is reflecting His heavenly kingdom on earth. One day, God Himself will establish His own kingdom, a kingdom that is coming. As we are working on earth, we are to let the world know that Jesus Himself is coming again to set up His eternal kingdom. Our lives should give hope to the fact that He is coming again.

Can the contemporary Church make the current welfare system obsolete? Yes, and the churches profiled in this book are reaching out and doing it, building indigenous leadership and empowering the poor in the process. I suggest that Washington pay close attention to the examples these churches are setting as they seek to fix our urban communities. Why? Because the following churches are the modern-day balms of Gilead, applying healing ointments to the myriad wounds of our cities.

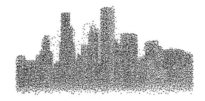

RECONCILIATION

All this is from God, who reconciled us to himself through Christ and gave us the ministry of reconciliation.
—2 Corinthians 5:18

Back to the Future

*Mendenhall Bible Church in Mendenhall, Mississippi,
and Voice of Calvary Fellowship in Jackson, Mississippi,
represent our roots in Christian community development
and in the ministry of racial reconciliation. Both have been
instrumental in laying a foundation for future congregations working toward Christian unity and holistic ministry.*

Home to Mississippi

By 1960, my family and I had returned home to Mississippi to minister to our people there. They were surprised to see us pull up with a
trailer attached to our car and our five kids with us. You see, no one
who left rural Simpson County for a better life ever came back. But we
knew this was the place God had called us to bring His message of love
and salvation.

Immediately, we went to work building relationships with local
farmers and neighbors, visiting churches and speaking in local schools.
Within only a few years, we had been able to share the gospel message
with thousands of elementary school children and high school youth in
their public schools by using Child Evangelism flannelgraph pictures.
We were also able to hold summer tent meetings with special preachers, Bible classes for adults in our newly formed Bible Institute, and
Christian camps for the local children.

From those early efforts, God brought us several key friends who
would help us throughout the years in the ministry. Many of these
were young people whom we had the immense privilege of leading to
the Lord. Who could have imagined the exciting ways God would
work in their lives?

Today, dozens of these same young folks have grown into effective leaders themselves in Christian ministry, reproducing their character, vision and work in the lives of the young people around them. This commitment to investing in and raising up indigenous leadership for Christian community development has always been the cornerstone upon which we built our work. I believe it is an integral part of the ministry of reconciliation God has given Christians.

Voice of Calvary Ministries

Because of the response from our new friends and neighbors during those first few years back home in Mississippi, we decided to focus our efforts on one town, so we formed Voice of Calvary Ministries (VOCM) in Mendenhall. Voice of Calvary was the original ministry in California, started by Dr. Jack MacArthur, that had sent me as a missionary to Mississippi. My Christian brothers in California prayed for us, sent us a small amount of monthly financial support to help in the work and also came to help in some of the summer outreaches. We were grateful for their faithfulness to us.

God was blessing us and our new friendships in the community so we formed our own independent organization called Voice of Calvary Ministries. We added the "Ministries" part because it best described our commitment to the holistic development of the work. We also organized Voice of Calvary Bible Institute to train leaders, and Berean Bible Church (now known as Mendenhall Bible Church) became the fellowship and discipleship arm. Mendenhall became a place where others could come and work out their faith with works.

I remember two young men in particular from that initial group of young people, Dolphus Weary and Artis Fletcher. Dolphus became a Christian at one of our tent meetings and Artis was converted at Prentiss Institute while we were conducting one of our Bible classes there.

I saw the tremendous potential both Dolphus and Artis possessed and the value in mentoring them, so I began treating them as if they were my own sons. We met together for Bible study, and worked together on construction projects and in youth camps. Once they graduated from high school, I encouraged them to attend college, maybe even seminary, while not-so-secretly hoping they would return to Mendenhall to lead the ministry. If they had training and an education, I knew they could be the key to changing Mendenhall for the better. They were our best natural resources.

I thank God that our investment paid off. After they received their college education, both Dolphus and Artis returned home to Mendenhall to help in the ministry. But not without some detours first.

Detours from the Call

Just before his wedding to Rosie in 1970, Dolphus had been selected to tour Asia with a Christian basketball team. While there, he was asked to join the sponsoring foreign mission agency full time. As Dolphus was praying and considering this offer, the answer came instead in another question, a still small voice asking him, "Dolphus, what are you doing ten thousand miles from home, when there are people in rural Mississippi who are trapped in racism, poverty and ignorance? Who will help these families?"

When Dolphus returned to California, he and Rosie discussed the possibility of moving home to Mississippi. They knew that hopelessness there seemed as thick as the Mississippi humidity, yet 75 percent of their peers were leaving the community for good. So the next year, having a diploma in hand, Dolphus and his wife, Rosie, decided to move back home. I was thrilled.

Artis, too, had done his share of traveling. When we first sent him out of Mississippi, he decided to attend Southern Bible Training School in Dallas, Texas. From there, he followed one of his professors, Dr. Wendell Johnston, to Washington Bible College in the nation's capital. He helped start a church in Maryland where he also married his wife, Carolyn. She had been studying at Los Angeles Baptist College, so the young couple moved back to California so she could finish school. All the while, Artis was working full time just to pay for school; no student loans or scholarships were available for him.

Once the Fletchers returned to Los Angeles, Artis was hired as a staff minister at Glendale Presbyterian Church under the direction of Dr. Bruce W. Thielemann. Artis then moved into a position as the interim pastor of an emerging interracial church called Vermont Avenue Presbyterian Church. By then, pastoring was providing a steady income for Artis and his family, so the thought of returning home to our poor community church in Mendenhall made him apprehensive. He also wasn't very excited about the intensity of the racial problems that existed. He knew if he returned he might be called on to put his life on the line. Still, when I called Artis to remind him of his commitment to return, he believed it was God's will. I was thrilled again.

Today, after 24 years of marriage and the accomplishment of raising three daughters, the Fletchers feel strongly about their hometown and Christian family at Mendenhall Bible Church. They are committed to "worshiping God, making disciples, reaching the total human being locally, nationally and worldwide."

Likewise, after three children, 25 years of marriage and extensive work as leaders in The Mendenhall Ministries, Dolphus and Rosie and their family can't imagine living anywhere else.

The Mendenhall Ministries

The growing leadership of Dolphus, Artis and their families persuaded us to put the work of VOCM into their hands, so we changed the name and the ownership to what is now known as The Mendenhall Ministries (TMM). As a result, TMM has continued to grow into an exciting nonprofit, nondenominational Christian organization whose sole purpose is to minister to the whole needs of people in the poor rural areas of south-central Mississippi.

After years of struggle against the institutional racism that has literally divided the small Southern town, the ministry now includes the Mendenhall Cooperative Health Center (which provides care for all local residents), an elementary school called Genesis One Christian School, the Community Law Office, a thrift store, adult-education classes, multiple youth programs and the Pastors' Development Ministry.

Dolphus is now serving as president of TMM, which means he is often traveling throughout the country, speaking to white and black audiences at churches and conferences about the reconciling work in Mendenhall, and recruiting summer volunteers for Christian community development projects. Artis serves as senior pastor of Mendenhall Bible Church where he oversees a staff of Timothy Keyes, Pastor Kevin Jones and other pastors, and a growing congregation of 200 members. He also works hard at providing a wonderful and unique ministry to more than 100 other pastors in Simpson County, organizing training seminars for them in pastoral care and community development, monthly Bible studies, theological education opportunities and an annual pastors' conference.

To say that I'm proud of these two "sons" would be an understatement! Why? Because of their work, the work of dozens of men like them and countless other faithful friends in the ministry, citizens of Mendenhall take pride in their community. Unlike the neighborhood in which young Dolphus and Artis grew up, streets are now paved, lawns are mowed, buildings and homes are cared for, and residents participate in a variety of businesses and town government functions. And, of course, hundreds of children are involved in numerous church activities, educational experiences and summer job and camp programs, all part of TMM's continued commitment to leadership development. (The next Dolphus and Artis are probably "in training" there even now!)

Planting Seeds in Jackson

Knowing that the Mendenhall work was in good hands, we decided to take those same seeds of Christian community development that were already producing good fruit and plant them 40 miles away in Jackson. We discovered that our people in West Jackson faced many of the same struggles as they did in Mendenhall, yet theirs were compounded with the problems found in most urban communities: poor housing, few job opportunities, high crime rates and so on.

Our mission quickly became clear in Jackson: to address the felt

"VOICE OF CALVARY MINISTRIES' PURPOSE IS TO DEMONSTRATE THE GOSPEL OF JESUS CHRIST THROUGH HOLISTIC MINISTRY AMONG THE POOR. WE SEEK TO ACCOMPLISH THIS THROUGH PROGRAMS WHICH DEVELOP INDIVIDUAL FAMILIES AND COMMUNITIES, EMPOWERING THEM TO REACH THEIR FULL POTENTIAL IN CHRIST."

needs of our new neighbors with the holistic love of Jesus while simultaneously developing a vision for a nationwide ministry of Christian community development. Really, it was here that the first seeds of our national organization known today as the Christian Community Development Association were watered.

Many of our Mendenhall young people also had come to Jackson to go to college at either Jackson State University or the local Christian college, Belhaven College. We wanted to continue nurturing them during their college days so we provided opportunities for them to serve in the community and to study the Bible.

We also started regular fellowship meetings and local outreach projects, developing a mission statement that reads: "Voice of Calvary Ministries' purpose is to demonstrate the gospel of Jesus Christ through holistic ministry among the poor. We seek to accomplish this through programs which develop individual families and communities, empowering them to reach their full potential in Christ."

During those times in the early 1970s, we, along with the help of several other friends, developed the Thriftco clothing store, a quality health care facility, youth programs and a housing renovation program. All the while, we talked about the idea of forming a church fellowship. You see, the way it usually works is that most Christians are sent from a church to establish some sort of ministry for the people in a needy area. But we were already ministering to the people and soon found ourselves discussing how to start a church.

Voice of Calvary Fellowship Is Born

We recognized that our little house Bible-study gatherings were beginning to take on the appearance of a neighborhood church. But we didn't actually begin to form our group into a church until we helped with the 1975 Billy Graham Crusade in Jackson. So Voice of Calvary Fellowship (VOCF), an interracial, nondenominational church, was born, largely as a result of our need to come together and largely because we wanted to point people from the Crusade to a congregation of Christians who would provide for them ongoing support and love in West Jackson.

From the start, we believed VOCF could be different from other local congregations. Here we were in the heart of the South, in the heart of a city, in the wild days of the mid-1970s. We believed we had a unique opportunity to witness to the world our biblical commitment to racial reconciliation according to the example of Jesus Christ. By 1977, we intentionally hired a white brother, Phil Reed, and a black brother, Romas McLain, to copastor the congregation. Along with both white and black elders, deacons and members who comprised VOCM staff and volunteers, the church began to grow.

Personal Growth and Blessings

Now, almost 20 years later, Pastor Reed is still the pastor at VOCF, where he and a team of loyal elders and deacons shepherd a congregation of some 200 black and white members. (Pastor McLain pursued another ministry shortly after the church was a year old.) After years of working with both blacks and whites, northerners and southerners, Pastor Reed believes several things must happen for true reconciliation to occur in a church:

- An early decision to maintain a cross-cultural worship and Body life that will sustain the congregation during difficult times;
- Affirmation of race and culture as important and relevant aspects of the members;
- Recognition that the reconciliation process never ends; and
- Ensuring multicultural leadership to speak to all members.

Recognizing these points didn't necessarily come easy for the pastor, though. After seven years of serving at the church, Pastor Reed was confronted by the fact that many black members were not being nurtured through his teaching. Consequently, he admitted his ignorance about black history, studied and began preaching messages that were culturally relevant. He says an unexpected blessing happened as a result: "I found some of my most inspiring models of faith and perseverance—black Christians such as Richard Allen, Mary McLeoud Bethune, Harriot Jacobs and Corporal James Henry Gooding. The culture was transforming me."

The Longest Short-Term Volunteer

To be sure, Pastor Reed had come a long way from his early years in Jackson. He had come to Jackson in 1974 from his home in Indiana, intending to serve only as a onetime summer volunteer and then return home. But the next summer came, and he found himself on staff with the ministry. The year after that, he became pastor of the church. He never left.

Phil's willingness to extend his short-term mission trip indefinitely paid off. He also met his wife, Marcia, in Jackson. He was assigned to pick up Marcia and other summer volunteers at the airport in June 1976. They worked together for the next few months, but by August, she decided to return to her home church, Peninsula Bible Church in Palo Alto, California.

A handful of Marcia's white friends had since moved to Mississippi to join in the work; however, Marcia spent the next year praying with friends and her pastors, Ray Stedman and Ron Richie, about the possibility of going back to Jackson. "I left after that first summer, convinced my service was through," she recalls. "But my theological world had been turned upside down. No one else was talking about justice and reconciliation. I had to go back."

Convinced that the witness of black and white Christians working together in the South was a powerful contemporary demonstration of God's love, Marcia felt stirred to respond. Her friends and pastors in Palo Alto encouraged her to go back to Jackson, and helped her raise support so she could return to full-time Christian work in Mississippi.

By the summer of 1977, Marcia left her home church, joined the VOCF staff in Jackson, and months later, married the young red-haired pastor. Today, Marcia serves as the Volunteer Services Coordinator for VOCM. She now recruits, corresponds with and trains other young summer volunteers like herself once they arrive. She works with 350 a year to be exact, coming from such faraway places as Sierra Leone, Nigeria, Rhode Island, Pennsylvania, Canada, Michigan and, of course, California. Marcia is also the mother of three children, helps with the youth at the church and is convinced she and her family "will be here for the long haul. Where else would we go? Though other churches are doing similar work, we would need the confirmation of our church family here before we ever thought about leaving."

The Reckoning Years

A statement of such loyalty can only come from years of tested allegiance. Marcia and the core members of VOCF have quite understandably endured some difficult trials in maintaining their commitment to racial reconciliation.

In 1983, the folks at VOCF experienced what longtime member and now *Urban Family* magazine editor, Chris Rice, called the "reckoning years." Specifically, the church planned a series of special meetings just to address racial issues and cultural differences so it could remain a reconciled church. For months, members and leaders came to intensely emotional weekly meetings to sort out their feelings, hopes, resentments and prayers.

"Those racial reconciliation meetings that year didn't always feel good. Some people, white and black, left the church as a result. But the core of 50 or so hung in there and endured confrontations that would have split most churches in half," Chris says.

I believe the VOCF became all the stronger because of those meetings. Anytime Christians get together and honestly talk about their differences in love, the whole Body of Christ becomes stronger for it. Although Vera Mae and I had already moved to California by then to "retire," I'm convinced those racial reconciliation meetings solidified the purpose of the work in Mississippi. The congregation developed a clearer picture of who they were to be, a vision that remains solid today and that serves as a powerful example to others interested in maintaining a long-term commitment to racial reconciliation.

Antioch Community Is Established

Either in spite of or because of those talks, another powerful example of Christian unity emerged. By the mid-1980s, a core of some of those same black and white VOCF members established an intentional living community in West Jackson and called it "Antioch." My oldest son, Spencer, his wife, Nancy, Chris and his wife, Donna, Gloria Lotts and her son, Kortney, along with other families and VOCM interns decided to share a huge 11-bedroom, 6-bathroom house on Robinson Street.

Now, more than eight years later, Antioch owns two houses next door as well, which serve as temporary quarters for interns and the offices of *Urban Family* magazine where Spencer and Chris work as editors. Nancy works as art director and several Antioch members (such as Christy Haas, Jennifer Parker, Helen Wambari, Elisha Risser and Danny Hill) work as the magazine team.

The Antioch community is "bursting at the seams," representing a rainbow of people. Of the children there, one is white, two are black, four are biracial (including three of my own grandbabies) and two are adopted. Says Spencer, "Life is full, but there's always an extra place at the dinner table if you're in the area."

Passing the Torch
The Antioch community is a wonderful extension of the VOCF family, a family that started way back in Mendenhall—a family that has, by the grace of God, influenced hundreds of lives for Jesus Christ.

One of those lives VOCM has influenced is Melvin Anderson, a 40-year-old graduate of Jackson State, who grew up with us in Mendenhall. My wife, Vera Mae, became his second grandmother, calling Melvin at college and praying for him through the years. When he married his wife, Thelma, they settled down in Jackson where he got a job as program coordinator at the local YMCA.

Soon, Melvin and his family started coming to services at VOCF. By then, Thelma had already joined the nursing staff at our health clinic. And though Melvin had grown up around Christians and a strong Christian grandmother who would read the Bible to him, he didn't make a serious Christian commitment until my son Derek challenged him to live for Jesus.

Soon after that, Melvin joined the VOCM housing staff, then under the direction of my dear friend and brother Lem Tucker. (Lem has since gone on to be with the Lord.) Lem encouraged Melvin, trained him in the ministry and instilled in him the same vision for Christian community development that had long sustained us. By 1991, Melvin became the third president of VOCM—I was the first and Lem was the second—and today he is an inspirational leader in both the church and in the community.

Melvin is a wonderful testimony of the ministry God has called us to. He represents the power of building indigenous leadership while proclaiming God's transcending love across racial lines. And he is a living example of the good that can happen when Christians are committed to each other as brothers and sisters and as a family, regardless of the most difficult circumstances that might come our way.

You see, Melvin lost his oldest daughter, Tarsha, two years ago in a car crash. Tarsha was a talented college senior, about to graduate with a degree in journalism from the University of Southern Mississippi. She also had a job waiting for her after she received her diploma.

When they learned of the tragedy of Tarsha's death, Melvin and Thelma were overcome with grief. But Pastor Reed, Marcia and other friends from VOCF immediately came to the Andersons' home. They stayed there around the clock, cooking, praying and crying with them. Their support and care were demonstrations of God's love to the hurting parents and their other three children.

Melvin is grateful: "I honestly don't know what we would have done without the love and support of my family at Voice of Calvary. But they have always shown me that I had a place to go, a place where I belonged. They were there for me when we lost our daughter, just like they always had been."

Taking It to the Streets

Both Mendenhall Bible Church and Voice of Calvary Fellowship are living proof of God's powerful love, a love that brings together black and white Christians even in a region of the country stained with a history of racism. From both churches, we see what can happen when Christians respond to the felt needs of their communities and are willing to work out and work through their differences for the sake of the gospel.

In Jackson and in Mendenhall today, both churches are well respected for their efforts in promoting holistic Christian community development along with racial reconciliation. Consequently, they serve as models to other congregations willing to commit themselves for the long haul to the reconciling work of God's kingdom.

What are some of the felt needs in your community? How could you and your church begin to meet those needs? Who are some of the young leaders in whom you could now begin to invest for the future of your ministry?

I pray God will reveal to you His vision for your life and your church in working toward Christian community development and racial reconciliation.

Of Partners and Process

*Two churches in Akron, Ohio, one black and one white,
are working together to show their city what happens when
Christian leaders dare to step across racial boundaries to
develop a friendship.*

Sunday Morning at Arlington Road Church of God

It is 8:15 A.M. Sunday morning. The royal-blue sanctuary of Arlington Road Church of God in Akron, Ohio, is filling up for the first worship service with handsome, friendly members of this predominantly black congregation. The 30-member men's choir is bellowing "He Took My Sins Away," and children are sitting obediently with their parents who, by now, are clapping and singing along with the choir's musical declaration.

As the organist plays her last note, Associate Pastor Dr. Diana Swoop walks to the podium. She prays a heartfelt prayer for the nations and the community, ending it with a sincere plea: "Out of all the things we might attain in this world, O God, we want to be connected to your Kingdom." A unified "Amen" brings the ushers forward as they pass a special offering plate for a scholarship fund for their college students.

The senior pastor, Dr. Ronald Fowler, then stands before his flock and preaches his three-point sermon: a challenging word to choose wisely the partners with whom we travel through life. If we "sleep with the enemy," he warns, it "creates bondage, causes blindness and cancels blessings." A warm smile spreads across the face of this compact, fiftysomething shepherd as he shares his final remarks of the service with his friends. "Nothing succeeds like obedience. It doesn't matter if people have a Ph.D. or a lot of money if they are still walking in darkness. Thank God there's always hope in the Scriptures." Quietly, the pastor prays and sits down as the choir starts up again with "The Lord Has Given Me Joy and Peace."

Sunday Morning at The Chapel

Not more than a few miles away from Arlington Road Church of God, hundreds of handsome, friendly white members enter a massive worship center at their nondenominational church known as The Chapel.

SOMETHING ATYPICAL IS HAPPENING

BETWEEN THESE TWO MEN AND THEIR

TWO PROMINENT CHURCHES, SOMETHING,

UNFORTUNATELY, NOT OFTEN ASSOCIATED

WITH BLACK AND WHITE CHRISTIANS.

SIMPLY PUT, IT IS CALLED "FRIENDSHIP."

At the first of four Sunday morning services, Chapel participants listen to the 100-member choir and orchestra as they are called to worship by another fiftysomething shepherd, Senior Pastor Knute Larson.

From the balconies to the front pews, people then join Worship Pastor Miller Cunningham as they sing choruses such as "Jesus, What a Wonder You Are!" and "There Is None Like You." After a special offering is taken for their urban ministry outreach, the tall, thin senior pastor approaches the podium. "When a church stops reaching out and caring about its guests, or forgetting the Cross," Pastor Larson admonishes, "it begins a slow death."

Pastor Larson then encourages his congregation to greet one another, and to sign up after the service for an Adult Bible Fellowship or a ministry project. His three-point sermon that follows explains the miracle of God's invasion into earth through His Son Jesus Christ, bringing with it a "sense of possibility, humanity and responsibility." A warm smile spreads across the face of this athletic-looking man as he shares his final remarks of the service with his friends: "Remember, 'saved' is still a good word if you're drowning." Quietly, he prays and sits down as the choir starts up again with "Good Christian Men Rejoice."

Friendship Between Black and White Pastors

It is a typical Sunday morning for both pastors and both congregations in this small industrial city of Akron, Ohio. Both men are recognized in the community as leaders with integrity; both churches are known for their numerous ministries and works throughout the city. Although both congregations are largely considered commuter churches, they are equally recognized as churches that consistently seek the welfare of the city. In short, both churches proclaim Jesus Christ as Lord, lift up His name and take seriously the biblical mandate to love God and to love their neighbors. One is a white megachurch, the other a large black community-oriented church; both are going about the business of their heavenly Father.

But something atypical is happening between these two men and their two prominent churches, something, unfortunately, not often associated with black and white Christians. Simply put, it is called "friendship." That's right—in a city not really known for anything but its tire factories and polymer research, Dr. Fowler and Pastor Larson are developing quite a reputation here for fostering cross-cultural friendships. Often, the two pastors can be seen together in 60-second spots on television playfully arm wrestling, while inviting viewers to visit their churches where they "wrestle over racial issues in a supportive, Christian environment." They can be seen together around town at business luncheons or civic events, speaking about racial reconciliation or unity in the Body of Christ or even their own relationship.

Quite intentionally, the two pastors have nurtured a partnership I consider an exciting example of what it will take to bring about reconciliation in our still highly segregated society. I have always believed that the whole Church must be a reflection and a model of the kingdom of God, demonstrating to the world the love that Jesus talked about in John 13:35: "By this all men will know that you are My disciples, if you have love for one another" (NASB). When this kind of authentic Christian love occurs across cultural lines, as it does in Akron, the world begins to notice, and ultimately, God receives the glory.

So with big hopes that their congregations, and other Christians, would do the same, Dr. Fowler and Pastor Larson went to work on their friendship four years ago. As veteran pastors of well-established churches—each with rich histories for ministry—the two had known of each other for years and would often run into each other at community events and interdenominational gatherings. But it wasn't until Pastor Larson met with Andre Thornton, the all-star first baseman from the Cleveland Indians, and six other pastors from Akron to discuss working together for the "physically and spiritually impoverished," that he realized the value of nurturing cross-cultural friendships. That meeting sparked in him a desire to do something more than just preach from the pulpit against prejudice and for racial harmony. He felt guilty that he had not done more. He knew better; his heritage had taught him more.

A Grandmother's Influence

Pastor Larson remembered the efforts of his humble Christian grandmother while he was growing up in Pennsylvania. She used to take young Knute with her to the Bible clubs she led for poor white and black children in the housing projects. She didn't care what color they were. She would tell her grandson, "They just need the love of Jesus." He also remembered attending church camps with black children, and memorizing verses such as Micah 6:8, "O man,...what does the Lord require of you but to do justice, to love kindness, and to walk humbly with your God?" *(NASB)*, and Matthew 7:12, "Do to others what you would have them do to you."

These experiences formed in Pastor Larson a sense of responsibility in caring for others by crossing cultural lines. But a few negative experiences also taught him important lessons. He was particularly struck with the indifference of some of his white parishioners at the church he pastored in Ashland, Ohio, before he, his wife, Jeanine, and their two daughters, Elise and Alison, came to The Chapel in 1983.

Pastor Larson recalls one incident where he invited an older deacon to join him as he made a "house call" to some visitors of their church. When a black family opened the door and invited Pastor Larson and the deacon into their home, the deacon was visibly surprised and awkwardly uncomfortable with the cross-cultural experience. The pastor shared about the church with the family, got to know them a little better, and finally, prayed together with them while the deacon sat quietly. When they left and got into the car to drive away, the deacon turned toward Pastor Larson and said, "Knute, you were good in there. You treated them just like regular people." The pastor stopped the car, horrified at the deacon's remark. "Do you know what you just said?" he asked the deacon. The deacon shook his head, perplexed by his pastor's question. At that point, Pastor Larson was stunned at how much work still had to be done in the area of racial unity in God's family.

Today, Pastor Larson openly admits that much of his initial effort for racial reconciliation came out of what he calls his "own white guilt." But he also recognized early on that white and black churches could mutually benefit from partnering relationships. So he took a chance, sat down with Dr. Fowler and confessed that not only did he desire for them to become better friends, but he hoped that Arlington Road Church of God and The Chapel could join forces in ministering throughout Akron as well.

"It was not a white church seeking to help a black church; it was us embracing each other. We were both so resourceful that we owed more to our neighbors who didn't have as much," admits the white senior pastor. And though his church of eight thousand members already had invested much time and money into a solid missions program, housed weekly Chinese and Vietnamese churches, and hosted hundreds of international students in one of 40 of their Adult Bible Fellowships, Pastor Larson knew they needed to do more. They needed to build friendships.

Like many black pastors, Dr. Fowler thought Knute's inquiry was nothing new. He had seen white pastors try to cross cultural boundaries before and give up just as quickly when the black brothers seemed resistant. The black brothers were not resisting relationships; they just did not want to be patronized. He had heard most of the black arguments that say, "The white folks will help you do something, but where are they when you need them just to be your brothers?"

To Dr. Fowler, the black religious experience could not conceive of a reconciliation to God that did not also include your neighbor. He had preached many times, "The message of salvation is never complete that allows a person to think that there can be reconciliation to God without being reconciled to his neighbor."

Strong Roots

Dr. Fowler had grown up in a fellowship where black and white Christians from Church of God congregations held an intense commitment to each other and lived their beliefs in joint revivals, pulpit exchanges, special cultural days and unity services. His father had served faithfully as the pastor at the church before he did and set a powerful example for young Ronald. Today, Dr. Fowler is proud to show off his black-and-white photographs from the mid-1950s: one of a local white pastor washing his father's feet, and another of his father washing the white pastor's feet at one of many joint services. They are symbols of the commitment to racial harmony Ronald has always known.

Sadly, though, Dr. Fowler also knows that his denomination bought into the church-growth theory that advocates homogeneous congregations to reach your own people. The Church of God denomination, he says, from the start had the vision for the whole family of God to be highly integrated. It had always been common to find Church of God white pastors working with black pastors, especially at traditional camp meetings in the 1930s and 1940s. But the new homogeneous thinking broke up harmony as the two cultures began to return to their separate groups, keeping Sunday as one of the most segregated days of the week. In spite of the Civil Rights Movement and the new laws for integration in the 1960s, the denomination did not take the opportunity to capitalize on the times.

But this Church of God pastor believes, "The homogeneous theory is too easy—it's too easy for us to naturally gravitate toward people who are like us. And integration asks so little of people; really, it asks only that you be civil. It cheapens the gospel because there isn't enough cost. Integration requires civility, but reconciliation requires crucifixion." Consequently, Dr. Fowler's church on Arlington Road has long held a commitment to reconciliation and social ministries.

The church operates a Senior Citizens community home called Arlington Housing Options Plus Elderly Services (AHOPES). It also sponsors evangelism outreaches and educational programs, such as the Arlington Christian Academy where more than 200 local children receive a quality Christian education and college scholarship funds. So because Dr. Fowler had naturally thought through these issues and understood the cost of reconciliation and community involvement, he was open to the idea of friendship that Knute Larson proposed.

Still, Dr. Fowler confesses today, he was a bit cautious when he first heard from The Chapel's senior pastor. Why? Because he perceived The Chapel as being more project-oriented while his own church was relationship-oriented. He also recognized that the attributes of their respective cultures—that is, that collectivism is an African ideal and individuality is largely a European one—might be too difficult to work through. But he believed, "Both ways of thinking are legitimate and need some way to be reconciled. These can be complementary." Besides, ultimately Dr. Fowler knew from his own experiences growing up that the rewards of his cross-cultural friendship would outweigh the challenges.

Forming "Allies"

So the two pastors went to work. They formed a ministry program and a church partnership to better address the social and spiritual needs of Akron. They called it "Allies," like the good guys in World War I. "We like the word 'Allies,'" says Pastor Larson. "We think it's a war underneath the surface in many hearts and many communities."

The two pastors then recruited dozens of people from their churches to work together and form specific committees to address issues such as tutoring, economic development, health care, family ministries, counseling and sports outreaches. At the same time, they encouraged the committees just to spend time together, talking, relaxing, praying and eating together to develop one-on-one relationships. The pastors hoped that natural relationships would be built as their people worked side by side in confronting the problems of the city.

The two leaders also decided to meet together once a month to discuss "business" and frequently to socialize. They and their wives get together regularly for dinner or to go to the theater. Though they both admit they would like to spend more time developing their personal friendship, they recognize how difficult it is because they are both extremely busy pastoring their churches and serving in numerous community efforts.

Dr. Fowler serves on the Akron school board as well as on the board for nearby Anderson College. Pastor Larson oversees a downtown business outreach called "TableTalk," as well as several media ministries.

As Dr. Fowler describes it, "Our relationship could be characterized as growing, still in its primordial stage in its development. We feel good about being with each other so there's no need to be defensive. And we like each other. All that is important for a relationship to have a chance at success."

The two pastors know that they have real challenges ahead, and by "owning up to the fact that we still have real racial problems in our society, I believe we're finding creative ways to deal with them. Allies is one way to deal with those issues."

Pastor Larson agrees: "Our church can't shift overnight but it can at least do something by partnering."

Other people have begun to take notice of the fruit of the pastors' friendship as well. In a series of award-winning articles on black-and-white relationships called "Coming Together," Akron's local newspaper, the *Beacon Journal,* profiled the pastors' friendship and their work with Allies. The headline read, "Learning to Love Like Brothers."

And as Associate Pastor Dr. Diana Swoop has watched the two men's relationship evolve, she has seen it become "one of mutual admiration, respect and brotherhood. They started out one seeking the other. But soon they realized they needed the other. In the process, they found both brotherhood and friendship."

Becoming "Brothers"

But another exciting story of brotherhood and friendship is taking place in Akron as well. Even before their pastors were working on their friendship, two local businessmen had put racial reconciliation on their personal agendas and went to work at the grassroots level. Ralph Gatti, a 37-year-old white businessman and lifelong resident of Akron, has nurtured an unlikely friendship with Bob Sturkey, a black 42-year-old former dentist.

The two Christian men knew of each other in high school. Ralph remembers watching Bob play basketball at the high school they attended, but they didn't meet until 1985 at a conference in Pittsburgh, Pennsylvania, where I was speaking on racial issues and Christian community development. Though Ralph grew up listening to the same Motown music Bob loved, he discovered from that weekend conference that something wasn't right in his life. He needed to initiate cross-cultural relationships.

"I found out I didn't have a handle on attitudes toward people who are different than I am," Ralph admits. "And when I recognized that was true of me, I felt compelled to deal with it from a Christian perspective. I saw it as a sin and needed to address it."

So Ralph and Bob became friends and eventually partners in the Gatti family's manufacturing business that Ralph operated. Bob sold his dentistry practice to come into business full time with Ralph. Soon they saw that their cross-cultural commitment strengthened both company sales and many opportunities for ministry.

"The success of our business partnership," says Bob, "gives us valuable credibility when challenging other businesses to use their talents and resources to bring about positive change in urban communities."

That's not all these two men's example has proven. I firmly believe this team of brothers has been instrumental in lighting spiritual fires throughout Akron. They see their business solely as a vehicle to building the kingdom of God in a variety of holistic efforts. Not only have they been deeply involved in Allies, they have also invested their own time and money into many ministries throughout the city and through their respective churches.

Ralph and Bob's ministries have included Urban Vision—a youth ministry in the predominantly black neighborhood called Elizabeth Park; Love INC—a clearinghouse of 800 volunteers from 25 local churches willing to donate their talents to help people in need; and Because He Cares—a group that addresses contemporary issues such as drug abuse, AIDS, violence and gangs through performing-arts workshops for African-American teens. And the two men can be credited with helping several other urban projects, Christian ministries and citywide events.

I believe Bob and Ralph provide an excellent example of what lay leaders can do to influence their cities for Christ. Their personal commitment and professional experiences have affected the Body of Christ in Akron in wonderful ways. For instance, when the two men helped put together a conference on racial reconciliation in 1987, they invited me to be the main speaker. Through that effort, we started to address the reconciliation issue to various church leaders throughout the community, including the two men's pastors from The Chapel and Arlington Road Church of God.

Businessmen Collaborate with Pastors

During that time, Ralph and Bob also started talking and meeting with their pastors. Ralph and his wife, Bonnie, had been active members at The Chapel for as long as Pastor Larson had been there. Though at one time Bob was also a member of The Chapel, he had always considered Dr. Fowler his pastor, the one who "mentored me, directed me and partnered with me." So they shared with their pastors their enthusiastic ideas for unity and racial justice in the Body of Christ, inviting them to functions, loaning them books, and praying for and with them. Consequently, their work together won the admiration of their leaders.

"To find two very competent and intelligent businessmen who are deeply committed to Christ and His church and to each other is rare," says the Arlington pastor (who also recently had the privilege of performing the marriage ceremony for Bob and his bride). A few years later, Ralph and Bob organized a major event called "Seek the Welfare of the City I." By 1994, they hosted at the Akron Convention Center "Seek the Welfare of the City II," where both my

"THE CHURCH IN THE BOOK OF ACTS...WAS NOT AVANT-GARDE, BUT THOSE BELIEVERS FOUND SOMETHING IN CHRIST THAT CAUSED THEM TO TRANSCEND THE BARRIERS OF CLASS, RACE AND CULTURE."

friend Thomas Tarrants III and I spoke, along with several other pastors, including Knute and Ron. These weekend conferences brought together hundreds of Christians from throughout the area, causing many of them to cross denominational, cultural and economic lines for the first time. Black and white businessmen began to meet together after that, ministries and churches began to network and personal partnerships began to form because of these rallies. As Ralph puts it, these meetings gave "average Christians the opportunity to look into other people's eyes to hook up with them and say, 'I could work with you.'"

At the same time, Bob and Ralph also became active members of our national organization, the Christian Community Development Association (CCDA). They visited with several ministries in other cities, attended workshops and observed organizational strategies. Now, Bob is serving as treasurer on our national board, Ralph is educating and recruiting local ministries to join, and the two have become powerful voices for the principles of Christian community development. They also took Dr. Fowler to visit Lawndale Community Church and CCDA headquarters in Chicago to share the vision with him.

Because of the partnership of Bob and Ralph, their pastors and the churches they attend, Akron is a city that is becoming known for its efforts to bring people together across cultural and denominational lines. Their combined efforts have helped foster many relationships there that have furthered the work of individual ministries as well as the issue of racial reconciliation.

Though all would agree that much work remains to be done, that they aren't anywhere near where they would like to be and that they are in process, the efforts of the four men have created an exciting momentum for the Holy Spirit to work. They reflect what Dr. Fowler would call something similar to "the Church in the book of Acts. It was not avant-garde, but those believers found something in Christ that caused them to transcend the barriers of class, race and culture. It was a divine compulsion to embrace the whole family of God, a nonnegotiable mandate that, thankfully, Jesus modeled for us."

So as Allies plans combined health fairs and evangelistic outreaches, as Pastors Fowler and Larson continue meeting monthly, as members from Arlington Road Church of God and The Chapel build their partnership, and as Bob and Ralph build their business and ministries, folks in Akron are beginning to see that the gospel of Jesus Christ really is good news.

As Dr. Fowler put it, "We're trying to make a difference in a long-standing history of racial isolation. We're trying to establish a Christian model that the community can use to pursue life at a higher level. It takes real strength to sustain a black-and-white relationship, to be vulnerable and to struggle with hard issues. As long as we stay programmatic, we won't have to talk about relationships."

And Dr. Fowler's friend Pastor Larson echoes his thoughts, "Churches have got to lead the way, especially evangelicals, because Christ is about reconciliation. If there is no power in God's spirit and mercy, then we're all only on the do-good level. Our goal is to work together and hope people will see us love each other in the process."

Taking It to the Streets

Both Akron pastors, along with Bob and Ralph, have developed friendships that are having far-reaching effects in their respective communities. I believe their example reflects the truth of John 13:35, "By this all men will know that you are My disciples, if you have love for one another" (NASB).

The deep love these Christian men have for each other is a testi-

mony to the power of the gospel, a gospel that not only reconciles sinners to God through Jesus Christ, but one that also reconciles men to each other, enabling them to become brothers in spite of cultural differences.

These men from Akron took small realistic steps to begin their friendships. They met for coffee, prayed together and encouraged each other through phone conversations. Why? Because they had made a commitment to God and to each other to advance the message of racial reconciliation. They thought about it, prayed about it, devoted themselves to it and allowed God to work through them to break down racial barriers.

If you are a pastor of a suburban church, how could you develop mutually supportive relationships with other pastors in your city to demonstrate this kind of reconciliation? If you are an urban pastor, how can you help encourage local suburban pastors in the ministry and work together? If you are a lay leader, how could you help your church become more culturally aware in working toward racial reconciliation? With which people could you pursue a friendship?

I pray that you will find creative, honest ways to nurture cross-cultural friendships for the sake of the gospel, and in the process, show the world God's transcending love.

A United
Christian Nations

*First Baptist Church of Flushing, in Queens, New York,
provides a dynamic picture of how people from various
cultures and races can work together in one Body for Christ.
To these leaders and members, Christian community
development is born from a deep commitment to racial
and spiritual reconciliation.*

Good News to *All* People

The man who first discipled me was a white man named Wayne Leitch. He was an elder at a Presbyterian church and the Child Evangelism teacher who had influenced my children. Wayne met with me often and used Acts 1:8 as a foundational Scripture for my life:

> But you will receive power when the Holy Spirit comes on you; and you will be my witnesses in Jerusalem, and in all Judea and Samaria, and to the ends of the earth.

From that passage, Wayne taught me two things: that the first work of the Holy Spirit is to make us witnesses, and that my Christian worldview for ministry should include going to Jerusalem, Judea, Samaria and to the ends of the earth. In other words, Wayne's early instruction formed in me a burden and a vision that the gospel must include crossing cultural lines for the sake of spiritual and racial reconciliation—that if it is not good news to *all* people, it is not good news at all.

First Baptist of Flushing: A United Nations

Imagine my delight, then, when in the early 1980s I first visited a group of black, white, brown and yellow Christians in Flushing, New York, trying to live out the good news of Acts 1:8. They formed the congregation at First Baptist Church of Flushing where women and men from dozens of different cultures were working side by side to show Christ's powerful love to their community. I knew when I saw them that this was what Wayne meant when he first taught me about being God's witnesses to the ends of the earth. And every time I return to Flushing, I see a little more of that vision lived out.

Walking into a staff meeting at First Baptist Church of Flushing is like walking into the United Nations. Representatives from countries such as South Africa, Peru, China, Brazil, West Indies, El Salvador, Philippines and the United States preside around a large oak table in the pastor's office, discussing strategies for change and empowerment for their people. With rich accents and lively, animated gestures, brown, yellow, white and black women and men exchange points and ideas. As each person speaks, the others listen with an unusual respect and intentional support not often seen in such diverse settings.

Observers would wonder about the friendly sentiment that resounds throughout this room, which resembles a professor's office more than a pastor's. The attitude here is no doubt as foreign in United Nations meetings as the people themselves. But nothing is political about this group; in fact, this diverse team of Baptist leaders almost prides itself on being politically incorrect in its goals and objectives for influencing its community. Though they are from different cultures, they are, after all, Christian leaders who represent a united congregation, reconciled to each other through their common faith in Jesus Christ. They just happen to believe that the Great Commission can be fulfilled, in part, right in their own backyard.

And they are right. Flushing, just a 30-minute train ride from Times Square in Manhattan, enjoys a diverse population of more than 100 cultures and several religions, including dozens of Islamic centers of worship that serve people from Egypt, Syria, Iran, Turkey, Pakistan and Africa. Although some neighboring mainline Protestant churches are experiencing a dwindling membership because of the cultural pluralism, the 140-year-old First Baptist congregation has seen a dramatic increase in the past 15 years. It has maintained an open-door policy, reflected in its "welcome" signs written in languages such as Arabic,

Farsi, Spanish, English and Urdu, which hang outside the church entrance on Sanford Avenue.

The Vision of the Pastors and Leaders

The reason for the church's growth? I believe it has everything to do with the sensitive, multicultural vision of the pastors and leaders, a vision that includes a vigorous, intentional commitment to racial reconciliation while addressing the specific social and cultural needs of the changing community that surrounds First Baptist. There is no question in my mind that Senior Pastor Russ Rosser and copastors Henry Kwan and Jorge Prado, along with their devoted staff of culturally diverse leaders, work hard in leading their English-, Spanish- and Chinese-speaking congregation to reach out to their neighbors for Christ.

My friends at First Baptist Church of Flushing show the world that there is no more powerful witness than a diverse but unified people who reflect the reality that they are one in Christ. Consequently, more than 1,000 people from every continent except Antarctica and Australia now participate each Sunday morning in the multicultural and multilingual fellowship.

Baptismal services at First Baptist often record converts from five of the world's seven continents represented. Together, they encourage all their members, says Russ, "to find out where the hurts are in the community and respond. If someone needs child care, food, immigration services, employment or counseling, we respond with a grassroots effort and needs are met by grass roots."

First Baptist's Rich Heritage

But First Baptist Church of Flushing has long been known for its rich heritage in cross-cultural, compassionate ministry. The church began in 1856 with a significant outreach to newly arrived immigrants, such as the Irish potato farmers who had traded life in Ireland for what they thought would be better opportunities in America. Then just prior to the Civil War, First Baptist leaders gave communion to black visitors, and by 1871 church records show the congregation welcomed its first black members.

In the 1940s, an intense missionary program was developed and in the 1950s, the church organized youth meetings on the street corners and Know-Your-Bible Clubs for teenagers. Through the years, First Baptist became known as an active, caring congregation that was influencing its community for Christ.

By the tumultuous 1960s, the church once again reached out to the community by adapting to the ever-increasing multiethnic, multilingual fabric of Flushing. A Spanish-language worship service was held and encouraged by laypeople such as Vincent Lopez, the church organist. Reverend E. Cruz was hired in 1966 to serve the Spanish Fellowship, and Reverend Paul Ho led the Chinese ministry.

Coming on Board

Though these ministries continued, along with an outreach to the Jewish community, the early 1970s brought an unexpected decline in ethnic membership. By 1978, having only 142 mostly white members left, the church asked Pastor Rosser to come on board. Russ left a homogeneous, white church where "they fought like cats and dogs" to be a part of First Baptist.

Although Russ had looked at the possibility of pastoring several other churches throughout the country, this one attracted him the most. Not only was it the smallest church, but he also saw here the most love out of any of the others. He was personally attracted to the multicultural heritage of First Baptist. His own concern for racial unity was born in his college days in Allentown, Pennsylvania. In the 1960s, he had started a Spanish congregation and hired a black musician to help lead their worship. Pastor Rosser was a natural fit for the Flushing congregation.

As a committed learner of cross-cultural ministry by the time he arrived, Pastor Rosser quickly recognized that his new church reflected only a smattering of the surrounding neighborhood. He asked the members if they should continue to cater to the declining group of traditional whites or if they would be willing to become a multicultural church again, one that reflected the dozens of ethnic groups that comprised the Flushing community. Though hesitant at first, the group agreed and began to realize, as Russ put it, "'The ends of the earth' according to Acts 1:8 had come to our doorstep."

When the church first discussed the issue of remaining homogeneous as opposed to becoming a heterogeneous congregation, Pastor Rosser remembered a passage in Isaiah 54:2,3 that he believed God had given to him:

Stretch out the curtains of your dwellings, spare not; lengthen your cords, and strengthen your pegs. For you will spread abroad to the right and to the left. And your descendents will possess nations, and they will resettle the desolate cities *(NASB)*.

Russ believed these verses from Isaiah directly applied to the international situation in Flushing, especially when he visited and saw the unity and potential among the lay leaders. He knew leadership would be the key to influencing the whole community, so he tapped into the existing ministries, affirmed the oneness at the leadership level and set about to bring people together. The key, he knew, was a diverse leadership that represented the needs of all the people in the community.

Multilingual Worship Services Added

So in 1979, the church called Jorge to lead Spanish and Portuguese services and Henry to conduct services in Mandarin and Cantonese. Reverend Bayer Lee also came along to assist the pastors with the

"THE CHURCH SHOULD BE

A PORT, NOT A FORT."

English-speaking Chinese members and with Christian education. Because of the diverse leadership representation, the joint congregations have been given opportunities for ownership at all levels.

Today, believers come from all cultural, economic, professional and religious backgrounds. Some new converts make radical breaks with their former Hindu, Muslim and Buddhist lifestyles to attend one of several multilingual services and to be nurtured in their new Christian faith through a variety of educational, supportive opportunities at the church.

Though many churches throughout the country merely rent space to non-English speaking congregations, First Baptist's unusual strategy includes all three groups as part of its one congregation, thriving on the rich diversity each brings to the fellowship. I believe it is significant to note that this church could have stayed homogeneous and comfortable in its congregation. Instead, the leaders recognized the strength of diversity and took seriously the mandate to be ambassadors for reconciliation. I believe this mandate is critical for the Church to recover so it can visibly demonstrate God's unifying love in an increasingly polarized society. Pastor Rosser put it well, "The Church should be a port, not a fort."

First Baptist: A Busy Port

First Baptist is one busy port. In addition to its multilingual worship services, First Baptist Church of Flushing has an Indian Fellowship, a Filipino ministry, numerous home-group weekly Bible studies in each language, Christian-education classes, prayer meetings, youth groups, parenting classes, a strong world missions program and choirs for each ethnic group.

Everyone is involved in ministry from the top down as the three cultural groups regularly combine for baptisms, joint worship services, multicultural dinners and other events. Last summer, First Baptist held a six-night community festival in the park across the street from the church. The festival included puppets, drama, testimonies, rap music, Chinese art displays and sermons translated in every language. The community responded well, as 300 people came to Christ.

"Basically, anywhere we can draw a crowd, we will to get the gospel out. As people see all colors, all people feel represented. The diversity is delightful because it makes us more sensitive," Pastor Rosser says.

Developing such diverse representation hasn't always been easy though; the church has had to work at it. But these friends have stayed committed to developing a theology of unity through reconciliation, a process that has continued to emerge since 1978. Their commitment to reconciliation has not been for the sake of political correctness nor to meet quotas. By intentionally hiring those who are culturally sensitive, Pastor Rosser and his team knew they would be fulfilling the gospel.

"We believe that because Christ died for all people, our proclamation of the gospel must be to all people. I guess we've had to incarnate the gospel," says Pastor Jorge. "We stay committed regardless of feelings. We respect and accept each other with all the differences and work together. It's our vision, not just some methodology."

A Sister's Commitment
Iris Holder, a longtime member and director of women's ministries, as

well as a retired chemist, attests to that commitment. As a black girl growing up in Flushing, she remembers the severe segregation of the community in the 1950s and 1960s. She and her sisters came to First Baptist as young adults when the congregation was entirely white. But they were welcomed, especially by the young people.

"Those young people led the way here and kept out the welcome mat for us," says Miss Holder.

In those days, restaurants often discriminated against blacks, but Miss Holder remembers her friends in the young people's group telling her they would "walk out with my sisters and me if the waitresses wouldn't serve us." Now, many of those early ambassadors for racial reconciliation are on the mission field bringing the good news of Jesus Christ to the nations.

The Disciples' Involvement

Today's young people have stayed true to their heritage. One young black woman named Miriam came to the church and quickly got involved in the college and career group, today known as "Christ's Disciples." The group was made up mostly of Chinese, Hispanic and white teenagers who welcomed and accepted Miriam as their new friend. Soon after she joined the group, she discovered she was pregnant from what was a one-night stand before she found Christ's Disciples. Instead of feeling alienated and afraid, Miriam was embraced by the young adults. They held a baby shower for her, built her up as a friend and also helped her economically. Miriam and her infant son today continue to be active members of First Baptist, thanks to the help of Christ's Disciples.

Americanized Apartheid

Dr. Prince Vuyani Ntintili, black South African pastor and Bible teacher at First Baptist Church, believes that the multicultural composition of the youth group at First Baptist provided a conducive social and spiritual environment for his daughter who was struggling with race issues at the time.

When the Ntintili family returned to the United States from South Africa, they lived in Summit, New Jersey. Their daughter experienced racism at the public school she was attending. This experience was poignant because in South Africa, a country known for its racist laws of apartheid, she was fully accepted and never experienced any racism. Whites in South Africa had reconciled themselves to the inevitability of coexistence between blacks and whites, so this was not much of an issue. So their daughter was accepted as a human being at the predominantly white school she attended when the family lived in South Africa.

But when the Ntintilis returned to the United States, their daughter experienced something she never expected; the color of her skin now became an issue. This shocked her and made her extremely bitter.

◼

"INCLUSIVENESS...IS NOT JUST SOMETHING THAT IS POLITICALLY CORRECT; IT IS, MORE IMPORTANTLY, BIBLICALLY AND THEOLOGICALLY CORRECT. IN THE BODY OF CHRIST, THERE IS NO DISTINCTION AND NO DISCRIMINATION."

◼

What further exacerbated their daughter's frustration was that she experienced undertones of racism from some young people at a church they attended in New Jersey.

The situation became so terrible at the church that when she and her sister sat in a certain pew, some white girls would move elsewhere. At first, she did not share this with her parents, but when they forced her to attend youth meetings on Fridays, she blurted out and said, "Why should I force myself into a group of people who do not appreciate my presence when my non-Christian friends make me feel accepted and wanted?" Consequently, Dr. Ntintili decided to join First Baptist Church.

"It is clear that racism is a cancer that destroys people, not only socially and emotionally, but it also has the potential of repelling them from the kingdom of God," says Dr. Ntintili. "That is what makes it so dangerous. Inclusiveness, on the other hand, is not just something that is politically correct; it is, more importantly, biblically and theologically correct. In the Body of Christ, there is no distinction and no discrimination. But this must be exemplified in our local churches. If not, we have falsified the gospel of Jesus Christ."

English: The Catalyst for Change
As the youth and the pastors are intentional in reaching out to those

who are culturally different, the church has been blessed to grow in a variety of creative ways. In the past, many newly arrived immigrants used to come to the church building just to hear the English language being spoken or to take an English class. Many didn't realize their lives would be changed by the Christian love they would experience there.

One Vietnamese woman, in particular, knows this to be true. Shortly after she began attending a few English classes at the church, she was abandoned by her husband. Suddenly, she was a single mother with a small son in a country where she barely knew how to survive. At least in her old country she had been a successful nurse at a small hospital, and so she could earn her own income. Now she didn't know how she was going to support her child, let alone learn the skills to pursue her career again. How could she get a United States' nursing license when she couldn't speak the English language?

When some families from First Baptist discovered the woman's dilemma, they took her in, helped her financially so she could learn both the English language and American nursing, and committed to watching her son so she could have more time to study. Not long afterward, she passed the licensing exam, found a job and an apartment, and is now working full time as a nurse, earning a reasonable income. Not only is she able to support her son, but she also gives regularly to the church so, as she says, others will have the same benefit and opportunities to succeed as she did.

The Pew-Ministers' Ministry

The Vietnamese woman's story no doubt indicates that this is a church that believes, as Miss Holder puts it, "Every person in the pew is a minister." Without the help of the "pew-ministers" at First Baptist, countless people would have felt hopeless and alienated. The Food Pantry, Crisis Pregnancy Center, several Salt and Light ministries, Teenage Basketball and many small accountability groups were initiated by members, not by the staff.

Members are encouraged and affirmed by pastors, deacons, elders and lay leaders to reach their community for Christ in whatever way they believe God is leading them. Such cooperative, active ministry illustrates the point that success really depends on healthy, visionary leadership that empowers the members to go "to the ends of the earth" and preach the gospel.

"Here we are committed to the notion that every believer has a gift from God and an ability to minister, and that requires training and empowering," says Hing-Tack Chen, chairman of the church board. "Pastors can't feel threatened by others' differences. Ours don't." Hing-Tack himself came to the church in 1972, thinking it was a Chinese church renting space from the Baptist congregation. But after he immigrated, Hing-Tack decided to join First Baptist Church of Flushing and quickly became involved in the church leadership. Why?

"I saw their vision to reach all people. I've seen this ministry evolve where the pastor is not indispensable, because the people are empowered. If we can have a church that reflects such differences, that is a great testimony to God. That is why I stay" Hing-Tack says.

Racial Reconciliation Commitment

And Hing-Tack is not alone in his beliefs. These leaders have spent many hours discussing, praying and studying together the issues inherent in racial reconciliation. "We are equal because we are different," says Pastor Kwan. "While some pastors in churches stifle the gifts of their members, here we try to discern what's best for everyone and delegate accordingly." They believe strongly in unity without uniformity—a process of growth they continually embrace while still acknowledging they haven't reached it because they are constantly growing.

Hing-Tack agrees: "Our commitment to maintain reconciliation is stronger than our personal views. We're very committed to the core of what we believe rather than the peripheral issues we sometimes think are important. We are in a theological evolution. Those with money don't rule here. But we know reconciliation is an ongoing process and we know God has His own agenda. Unity in the church is more important than anything."

Mission Trips Help Maintain World Vision
Such commitments extend far beyond the church's staff meetings and worship services. Each year, the pastors and leaders take teams on short-term missions trips to keep their world vision fresh. In places such as Hong Kong, China, Hungary, Russia, Brazil, Ecuador and El Salvador, the teams have worked with a variety of mission agencies, as well as with churches in other parts of the world. They are partners with InterVarsity Christian Fellowship, International Students Inc., Sudan Interior

Mission, Africa Inland Mission, the Conservative Baptist Mission to the Americas and Conservative Baptist International.

The church's missions commitment reflects its philosophy, one that should challenge others to do the same. Says Pastor Kwan, "The church as a whole has to be encouraged to send pastors and teams into the world and see it will benefit everyone. That will challenge them and renew their zeal. How can you change a church if you don't send a leader to Africa or Harlem? The vision of leadership needs to understand the agenda of God. Churches that hold, never gain. The more you give, the more you gain."

Seminary of the East

So the church put its money where its collective mouth was and took the role of leadership so seriously that it started a seminary. The Seminary of the East began in 1985 when Pastor Rosser helped found it as an alternative training center to traditional seminaries. Pastor Rosser and his colleagues believed traditional seminaries too often taught theological issues without the hands-on experience needed to accompany the student's newly acquired knowledge.

The goal of the Seminary of the East is to develop servant-leaders by providing them with academic training in the context of urban ministry. Students who are already in ministry are asked to receive the affirmation of calling and the spiritual support of their home churches to attend the Seminary of the East, while simultaneously maintaining active ministries. This way, the congregations and the leaders both benefit from the partnerships. The seminary then develops internship agreements by which the church provides two mentors to oversee the internship. Student and mentors then meet weekly to assess growth in character and ministry skills. Such a program gives leaders an opportunity to remain in their home context while staying under the guidance of their local pastors or leaders.

When Pastor Rosser first brought the idea of the Seminary of the East to First Baptist leaders, they quickly affirmed it, put money aside to assist in it and volunteered their facility as one of three campuses for the Seminary of the East (the other two are in Philadelphia and in Worcester, Massachusetts.) At one time, First Baptist had 15 people playing active parts in seminaries across the country. Now, at least 8 students from the church are at the seminary while working in local ministries. And more than 125 churches throughout the northeast are committed to supporting the seminary to provide tailor-made, graduate-level training for urban ministry.

Students are required to maintain personal spiritual lives, active ministries and challenging intellectual commitments in the context of their personal calling. More than one-third of the total 200 students are people of color, and many of the students come from professional backgrounds—doctors, pilots, educators—who now are, as Pastor Rosser, president of the seminary, says, are "learning truth in action."

The Seminary of the East is a natural extension of First Baptist's commitment to racial reconciliation and social ministry. As Dr. Paul de Vries, New York Center Seminary dean, says, "Racial reconciliation won't happen until leaders are committed to it. That's why we require reading like Dr. Martin Luther King's *Strength to Love* in addition to ongoing discussion and experiences that promote it." Consequently, students from churches such as First Baptist of Flushing (73 percent are from other denominations) come to the Seminary of the East with an intentional commitment to biblical reconciliation, spiritual formation and compassionate ministry. Fifty-four of the 55 graduates have been placed in full-time ministry throughout the world either on the international mission field or in an American urban community.

I believe the Seminary of the East and the staff and congregation at First Baptist in Flushing serve as a model for the kind of leadership development to which I have always been committed. It applies church-based training for men and women and provides mentoring opportunities in a holistic ministry setting, while maintaining a deep commitment to racial reconciliation—the very principles of the gospel. I thank God for men such as Pastor Russ Rosser who had a vision, shared it with Henry, Jorge and their other leaders, and now work together to train pastors and church leaders for practical Christian community development. This church and seminary can teach us how to do ministry as God intended.

Mostly, though, we need to recognize that First Baptist Church of Flushing was not satisfied with the homogeneous church-growth model so many American suburban churches have followed. Instead, they have found a creative, cooperative way to affirm all people, cultures and languages while proclaiming the good news of Jesus Christ. There is one unifying congregation in Flushing and one common treasure. As one member put it, "If God's Church is to be *the* Church, we've got to yield to the Holy Spirit. It's the Lord who brings us together."

Taking It to the Streets

Racial reconciliation is the backbone of First Baptist Church of Flushing, New York. Here, believers view their cultural differences as opportunities to strengthen their influence and witness in their surrounding community. They enjoy the unique gifts and attributes each leader and member brings to the congregation; to them, cultural diversity is as natural as the air they breathe.

But these people also know working together is not always easy. By having a deep commitment to respect and biblical unity, they know they can conquer any struggle their cultural differences might bring. First Baptist Church of Flushing really does reflect the global faces of the whole Body of Christ. Consequently, their church is growing, their lives are changing and their community is experiencing the powerful love of Jesus, a love that breaks and transcends cultural and economic barriers.

How can you be committed to racial reconciliation? What steps can you take to promote unity among Christians living in your community?

I pray that you and your church will experience the blessings of racial unity and cultural diversity, becoming powerful witnesses for God's transcending love.

RELOCATION

The Word became flesh and made his dwelling among us.
We have seen his glory, the glory of the One and Only, who
came from the Father, full of grace and truth.
—John 1:14

5

Daddy, Are You Going to Be a Sermon Today?

Lawndale Community Church in Chicago, Illinois, is a small, inner-city church making a big difference in its neighborhood. It is an exciting testimony to the influence black and white Christians can have when they relocate to the city to work together for Christ.

A Daughter's Challenge

One bright Sunday morning, almost 12 years ago, four-year-old Christie Casey was getting ready for church. It was an exciting ritual for the enthusiastic young girl: Each Sunday morning she would put on one of her favorite dresses, share a hearty breakfast with her father, mother and baby sister, Patrice, and then play in the living room while her family got ready. The Caseys always went to church; they had to because Christie's dad, Carey, was a pastor.

This particular fall morning, though, the young girl watched her dad with four-year-old curiosity as he sat quietly on their family sofa, praying and studying the Bible, organizing his final thoughts for the morning service. She watched his strong, slender hands point to verses and jot down notes on a yellow pad of paper; she saw his eyes close in reverent prayer. She tried with all her youthful energy to be patient as Pastor Casey finished preparing his sermon. But Christie's excitement could not be contained. After a few eternal moments, the little girl sprung across the room, pounced onto her daddy's lap, put her face just inches from his and asked, "Daddy, are you going to *be* a sermon today?"

Today, Pastor Casey laughs as any proud parent would when he recalls the incident with his daughter Christie. But he knows with certainty the power and truth behind his daughter's question. Many times since, he has remembered little Christie's challenge, realizing that being a Christian is much more than just talking from a pulpit on Sunday mornings. It is living out the power of the good news in a practical, daily lifestyle. It is demonstrating God's love in visible, creative ways.

Sharing Lifestyle Sermons

Yes, my friend Carey Casey knows that the witness of his everyday life for Christ as a caring pastor, as a faithful father and husband, and of course, as a friendly neighbor, communicates much more than any sermon he preaches on Sunday morning.

That's why Carey and Melanie, his wife of 18 years, their two daughters and young son, Marcellus, left a comfortable, middle-class lifestyle in Kansas City to join white veteran pastors, Wayne and Anne Gordon, at Lawndale Community Church in one of Chicago's toughest inner-city neighborhoods. For three years now, the Caseys and the Gordons and their families have worked side by side, sharing "lifestyle sermons" with their neighbors, sermons proclaiming the truth that God's love transcends black and white differences and breaks down cultural and economic barriers. Their friendship is living proof.

The two men meet each morning for prayer, Bible study and fellowship, where they speak into each other's lives. Consequently, as Carey puts it, "We back each other and enhance each other's credibility with the different cultures."

The two pastors' wives work together to coordinate a variety of women's ministries at the church. Their children play and worship together, and both families often share vacations and holidays with each other. I believe the special relationship between the Gordons and the Caseys, as well as their cooperative leadership of the many ministries of Lawndale Community Church, reflect holistic Christian community development at its best. Why? Because not only do both families, along with their church family, share a deep commitment to racial reconciliation, but they also believe that the good news of Jesus Christ's transforming love provides lasting hope for all people in all situations.

The Coach

Wayne understood these truths even as a young Wheaton College graduate when he first started his inner-city ministry in 1975. He had been hired to teach and coach at Farragut High School in Lawndale and made a bold decision to move into the neighborhood, becoming one of the only teachers, white or black, who actually lived in the same community as his students.

To me, Wayne has always been the all-American boy: athletic, competitive, bright, enthusiastic. But I believe his athletic, competitive spirit has helped to shape in him a confidence where he's not easily afraid of the people around him. People see him warmly as "The Coach." He can be effective around anyone because he's not threatened by people. I believe that's part of where his stamina has come from, a stamina that has enabled him to stay in Lawndale for almost 20

■

STAMINA, DEDICATION AND VISION ARE ALWAYS

REQUIREMENTS FOR ANY CHRISTIAN WHO HAS

RELOCATED TO A GHETTO.

■

years, surviving at least 11 break-ins in his home and numerous cross-cultural challenges. Stamina, dedication and vision are always requirements for any Christian who has relocated to a ghetto. Wayne has maintained all three in Lawndale.

As a young coach, Wayne received some weight-training equipment from the Chicago Bears and began a Bible study in a local storefront for his high school students. Now, 20 years later, the Bible study has grown into a 500-member multiracial church located in a renovated factory. Growth has occurred despite the fact that the Lawndale community has seen its population decline by half during the past 30 years. The remaining residents have watched most businesses, churches and families abandon Lawndale for better opportunities. To best meet the felt needs of its troubled urban neighborhood, Lawndale Community Church, led by Wayne, saw those problems as ministry opportunities and went to work.

I believe part of the proof of Wayne's early efforts has been in the leaders he's helped develop; some of whom came from that first Bible study and now are active leaders at Lawndale Community Church. Today, they have plenty of opportunities to get involved because the church now includes an active multifaceted, evangelistic youth center and gymnasium, a comprehensive health clinic, a housing rehabilitation ministry, counseling and job-training programs, family events and an overall staff of about 135 employees.

A Success Story

But Carey and Melanie Casey didn't move to the neighborhood because they needed to be a part of another successful ministry such as Lawndale Community Church. They were already familiar with success. I knew that when I first met them as a young couple dating at the University of North Carolina in Chapel Hill. As college students from good, small-town families, they were confronted early on with the attainment of success as well as with their responsibility to be positive role models. Both were greatly blessed with a rich Christian heritage and were taught as they grew up that they were not second-class citizens. Melanie's father even went to school with Dr. Martin Luther King Jr.

Carey and Melanie were also taught that the Bible says, "To whom much is given,...much will be required" (Luke 12:48, *NKJV*), and they understood its application to their individual lives. The two had always had a desire to get a good education, to travel, to be married and to minister God's love to those who didn't know Him. Carey claims he pursued Melanie at college because he knew "she loved God more than she loved me." After graduation and a wedding, they became fully convinced of God's call for their lives and felt the need to get more training. The Reverend Billy Graham offered to pay their way to seminary, and so the young Caseys entered a lifetime commitment to full-time Christian ministry.

Carey eventually worked his way to the Fellowship of Christian Athletes' national headquarters in Kansas City to become their national urban-ministry director, as well as a chaplain for the U.S. Olympic Team and several professional football teams. The Caseys became friends with people such as Herschel Walker, Tom Landry and Reggie White. Obviously, the family was settling well into the Kansas City lifestyle. Melanie was enjoying a fulfilling teaching position at a local elementary school, their children were doing well in their comfortable suburban neighborhood, and offers were coming in from all over the country all the time for the Caseys, affirming their talents and gifts and asking them to join this ministry or that church or to teach at such and such a school. They had made it, they thought, and they had no plans of moving. This was home.

Until Wayne Gordon called. Recognizing the need for a well-respected, well-educated black pastor to lead the predominantly black congregation at Lawndale Community Church, Wayne suggested he and his wife, Anne, step into another role as outreach pastors so Carey and Melanie could become shepherding pastors in the Chicago ministry. Suddenly, Carey was torn. Melanie understood Carey's passion to serve in the city but was worried about their children. All three kids told their parents there was "no way" they would ever want to live in Chicago. Still, the family felt led to visit Lawndale to interview, and after only a week there, the children found it difficult to leave. "We knew if God wanted us here, He would have to change the children's hearts," Melanie recalled. And God did.

An Atypical Move

So the Caseys, a typical, educated black urban-professional family, decided to make an atypical, life-changing move and relocate to one of America's toughest inner cities. Though others still think they are crazy for choosing to live in a neighborhood where most families are trying to get out, the Caseys believe this is exactly where they are supposed to be.

The transition was not necessarily easy for the Caseys; transitions never are. When they first moved into Lawndale, many neighbors had never seen a moving van. "Wait till you're broken into. Then you'll be poor like us," one neighbor told them. Some mocked them for talking "white," and the children weren't sure what to expect each time they walked outside their new home.

Still, the family has no regrets. "We went because God sent us," says Carey. "And we're ministered to because we're here. We're learning so much, especially as we've helped people and provided hope."

The move also meant that the Caseys were suddenly confronted with gun shots, drug dealers and loud music instead of the quiet, predictable routine of their former suburban community in Kansas City. The streets in their new neighborhood were dirtier, the houses older and the neighbors noisier. The house they moved into was next door to a drug house where six families lived; it had more traffic than a bus station. Just choosing this particular street made a serious statement, even to the people of the church. But the benefits, the Caseys say, have outweighed the changes.

Explains Melanie, "We've been helped just as much, if not more, since we've been here. It's like a big family. Here I actually know my neighbors. And every time I go to the grocery store, or Carey gets caught in a meeting, our kids have always been taken care of. It's not just that we're pastors. We're neighbors."

Building Trusting Relationships

As one of the few intact families on their block, the Caseys have built trusting relationships with their new neighbors in small ways, whether it is Carey and Marcellus picking up trash, Patrice and Christie inviting other kids to church or Melanie simply waving at the elderly woman next door. "People in the community now know us more as a family than as individuals," says Carey. "Even when my son and I pick up paper or work in the yard, the other kids want to help because it looks like fun."

The Caseys have been able to "be sermons" in a variety of ways, providing a wonderful compliment to the Gordons' influence. Melanie remembers a little neighbor girl who stopped her one morning outside their home. She noticed Melanie's diamond wedding ring and asked her about it. "You two aren't really married, are you?" The little girl had not really known many people who were married; most of her neighbors and her own family just had moms, and daddies didn't come around very often. She couldn't believe her new neighbors actually got married. Melanie assured her they had married and took the opportunity to tell her about Carey, their wedding and God's plan for families. It also made Melanie realize the influence their presence could have in their new neighborhood.

"The Gordons have been a great role model here but they are white and, to these kids, white people are supposed to have a family," says Melanie. "Our family shows them something different than what they are used to. In fact, just being a family here has made a difference. Now people miss us when we're gone." A teenage girl who lives across the street told the Caseys she wants a family like theirs when she gets older.

In a neighborhood where many of our men are either absent, incarcerated or dead because of violence, Carey's mere presence is also an inspiration. Once Carey went to get the family car washed. Bradley, a neighbor who often struggled with alcohol, was working at the car wash. As he saw Carey drive up, he yelled to the other workers, "Okay, guys, take care of this car because this here's my pastor."

Carey smiled at Bradley because he knew exactly what Bradley meant: You see, Bradley has *never* been to Lawndale Community Church to hear Carey preach. But he knows that Pastor Casey will always listen to him whenever they see each other on the street. He knows that Pastor Casey is one of the only people who always says to Bradley, "Hey, man, it's good to see you."

Family Life a Blessing in the Neighborhood

"People see a black man who lives with his wife and children and loves and cares for them," Carey explains. "Our neighbors see us discipline our kids. They hear them say 'Yes, sir' and 'No, sir.' That makes a difference."

One elderly neighbor woman rarely left her home before the Caseys moved in. She never thought it was safe to come out. The Caseys hardly knew she existed until one day when they were out working in their front yard. The woman saw them, came over and said, "I've been watching you since you moved in and wanted to tell you I'm glad you're here. Just to see your family come and go has been been a blessing to me." The Caseys were as surprised to see her as they were to hear her comments. They didn't even know her name let alone what her own family life was like. But they knew that simply by being themselves, they had been given another opportunity to "be a sermon."

The Caseys' own perspective of family has also been expanded since they came to Lawndale Community Church. "In the suburbs, we never felt the sense of community we do here. We had a neighborhood open house for Christmas in Kansas City and people came who had lived there 20 years but had never met each other," recalls Melanie.

The move has brought them closer together as a family as well; they are convinced that God brought them to Lawndale for their own good as a family. For instance, when their car was broken into by a drug addict shortly after they arrived, they cried together as a family and prayed that "God would help the man who did it." "Living here has tested our faith as a family," says Carey. "Every day we walk out our door, we put into practice our belief that God is our protector."

Lawndale Community Benefits Through Programs

While the Caseys' own family has been strengthened as a result of their move, so too, has the family at Lawndale Community Church. The Caseys' presence is felt at all levels. Carey has helped organize men's groups in addition to preaching each Sunday and pastoring throughout the week. Though Melanie works part-time as a librarian at a local school, she helps with Lawndale Community Church's tutoring and education and the Kingdom Women's Bible Studies. Christie has developed into a leader in the youth group, and she and her sister, Patrice, both sing in the choir. The entire family is active in one of the many programs at the church.

Through the Caseys' and the Gordons' influence, Lawndale Community Church has evolved into a powerful model of Christian community development, a model that I know is having far-reaching, holistic effects on its troubled neighborhood. The church has literally become a safe place of refuge for the children, where recreational activities are constant and an after-school tutoring program equips high school students for college, while elementary school children are helped with their homework.

Lawndale Community Church's members established the College Opportunity Program, where eighth-graders commit themselves to a five-year program of twice-weekly study sessions at Lawndale Community Church's Learning Center. The students are also required to maintain a 2.5 grade point average if they want to receive the $3,000-a-year, four-year college scholarship that the College Opportunity Program offers. Many of the kids who come now are talking about college because, as Anne says, "The younger ones see the older high school kids thinking and talking about going." About 40 of Lawndale Community Church's youth are enrolled in college each year—that's not bad considering the 50-percent high school dropout rate in the neighborhood.

A Passionate Purpose

Precious Thomas leads the Learning Center, where computers and colorful posters can be seen everywhere. She oversees volunteers and children daily as the students receive instruction about computers, math, reading and, of course, the Bible. Precious is passionate about her purpose and makes every effort to provide the children with creative opportunities for spiritual and academic growth, including frequent trips to the ballet, musicals and museums.

Precious believes that by providing quality programs in a positive environment, the center is helping create healthy people. "I try to make this place beautiful in every way for my babies because I love them," says the enthusiastic director, whose smile transforms her face. Additionally, she believes the center should be a safe place that reflects African-American culture and is used to build positive self-esteem. Nothing about this Learning Center is boring; if it were, says Precious, "We'd lose the kids. I do everything possible to make things fun for them. They deserve it."

Lawndale Christian Health Center

If the children catch colds or their families need medical attention, they can go to Lawndale Community Church's full-service medical center, where dozens of professional health-care workers are employed. Each month, more than 4,000 people from throughout the community receive quality treatment at a minimal cost. Since its opening in 1984, the Lawndale Christian Health Center has long been recognized as a clinic that provides "a Christian witness while enhancing the quality of health care in North Lawndale."

Comprehensive community-based primary health care is given, including speciality-care referral, prenatal, well-child, health education, dental, family, pastoral and HIV counseling. The Health Center also includes rotations for nurse practitioners, senior medical students and residential opportunities. And many of the doctors and nurses who work there also attend Lawndale Community Church; by merging their faith with their profession, they too, are "living sermons" to the same children they care for throughout the week. Their influence is beyond measure.

Coming Back

Richard Townsell is one former Lawndale youth who has been affected by the testimony of the professionals who have offered their services to the community. During a summer leadership-development program, Wayne Gordon first introduced Richard to a variety of black authors. "Those books started me thinking about how I could contribute to my community; before that, I was only focused on making money," Richard recalls.

After Richard graduated from Northwestern University, Wayne offered him a job as executive director at the Lawndale Christian Development Corporation, an organization dedicated to economic development, housing and education. Richard had to give up a comfortable position as a suburban school teacher to accept Wayne's offer. "I realized that if I wasn't part of the solution, I was part of the problem," Richard explains.

Richard now oversees a staff of nine as they minister in a variety of ways to the community where he grew up. Lawndale Christian Development Corporation has rehabilitated numerous abandoned buildings and made them available to first-time, low-income homeowners in the community. Dealing with at least 15 multifamily rental units, 72 single-family homes, and workshops to teach home-ownership skills, Richard and his Lawndale Christian Development Corporation staff are busy offering essential solutions to develop Christian community in the Lawndale neighborhood.

In 1993, they also began the Imani (which means "faith" in Swahili) Job Training Program, where about 200 adult students from throughout the community have been taught interviewing skills, discipline values and employment tips. To date, more than 50 people from Imani have found jobs because of the training they received.

Lawndale Church Restores Credibility

Certainly, job training, medical care, education and housing are important components to the influence Lawndale Community Church is having on its neighborhood. It has also helped restore the credibility of the overall Christian Body that was lost when Christians abandoned their responsibilities in the city. As Wayne points out, "The secular world supports ministries that help people with their physical and mental needs, especially if the church tackles problems no one else can or will." I believe these holistic ministries are crucial in obeying God's call to the poor and in restoring the Church.

Developing the Family of God

But it is the emphasis on developing the family of God that makes

Lawndale Community Church's efforts in these other areas especially significant. Consider the following: Lawndale Community Church's teenagers often volunteer to baby-sit younger children so their parents can go out on dates; 40 to 50 Kingdom Men meet weekly for prayer and intense Bible study; seminars on how to minister to family members are held frequently; "Friday Night Live" talent shows, rap concerts or carnivals are held once a month, where 600 to 700 fathers,

LAWNDALE COMMUNITY CHURCH'S MOTTO IS:
"WE DEVELOP PEOPLE, NOT PROGRAMS."

mothers, friends and children pack the gym; "Ebony, Ivory and Harmony" meetings are held quarterly, where black and white Lawndale Community Church members meet individually and then discuss racial and spiritual issues to bring to a joint Harmony meeting, and share communion. At each Sunday morning service, Pastor Casey shares the pulpit with members as he asks individual teenagers, single parents and couples to do the Scripture readings from the Old Testament and New Testament in front of the whole congregation.

The nontraditional pastor doesn't wear a gown, but he does preach the same gospel as his white partner has for 20 years. By doing so, they've challenged racial myths and ministered to the whole community. Between prayer meetings, home groups, Bible studies, and outreach and community service, God's family at Lawndale Community Church is being developed.

The church's motto is: "We develop people, not programs." Its foundational Scripture is from Matthew 22:37-39: "Jesus replied, 'Love the Lord your God with all your heart and with all your soul and with all your mind.' This is the first and greatest commandment. And the second is like it: 'Love your neighbor as yourself.'"

National Influence

While they continue to influence their neighborhood through the local ministry of Lawndale Community Church, the two partners also are having a national influence. Wayne is the cofounder with me, as well as the president, of our Christian Community Development Association (CCDA), a national network of urban ministries that has 4,000 individual members and 350 organizations in more than 40 states committed to reconciliation, redistribution and relocation. Anyone who has been to a CCDA national conference knows that The Coach's leadership and enthusiasm is exciting and contagious. And Carey continues to play a critical role in the development of urban youth ministry by serving on the national board of directors for the Fellowship of Christian Athletes. His vision for reaching young athletes in America's cities is a crucial addition to the 40-year-old sports ministry.

Lawndale Church Empowers People and the Community

Because of people such as Wayne and Anne, Carey and Melanie, their families and the other friends there, Lawndale Community Church is a great place of hope in that it empowers people and has created an expectation of empowerment for the community. Indeed, they are redeeming the Lawndale community along Ogden Street for the glory of Jesus Christ.

I thank God for what He has done with Wayne and Carey and how he has used them in Lawndale and CCDA. These leaders exhibit a mark of greatness in that they know how to listen and to take good advice, and they have a sense of determination, virtue and character that they have passed on to many others. I pray that their own children will pass on the good work God has begun at Lawndale Community Church, becoming themselves "living sermons" to their neighbors.

Taking It to the Streets

Relocating to a poor urban neighborhood meant for the pastors at Lawndale Community Church that their lives would become instant sermons. They discovered that how they treated their wives, children and neighbors would communicate more than any sermon they preached and would have more influence than any Christian program they hoped to coordinate. But they also knew that a relocated lifestyle would not be easy.

Still, the struggle has been worth the rewards for my black and white brothers at Lawndale. Because the Caseys and the Gordons, along with their colaborers at Lawndale Community Church, have committed themselves to developing their community for Christ, they have seen the blessings of God's transforming love. Whether it is in the life of a young boy who is suddenly doing better in school because of the church's after-school program, or in the family who got back together because of their counseling services, or in the black neighbors who have a better perspective of white people because of their efforts for racial reconciliation, these Christians in Lawndale are making a big difference.

What sermon has your life been preaching lately? How could you make a personal commitment to Christian community development in your city?

I pray that God would empower you to live a life worthy of the gospel, while showing people the power of His transforming love.

6

Holy Ground

*"God called to him from within the bush, 'Moses! Moses!'
And Moses said, 'Here I am.' 'Do not come any closer,' God
said. 'Take off your sandals, for the place where you are
standing is holy ground.'" This passage from Exodus 3:4,5
reflects the unique thinking of one church in Denver,
Colorado—a church whose very name, Church in the City,
defines its mission while showing what exciting things can
happen when suburban Christians allow God to lead them.*

For the Glory of the Lord

Denver's downtown YMCA isn't really known for its baptismal services. But once every third month, the indoor swimming pool is rented out for the evening and 50 or so urban visitors come for a time of dunking, contemporary worship music and Christian fellowship. They come in all ages, colors and shapes to watch friends and relatives profess their new-found faith in Jesus Christ. They come to what pastors of Church in the City call the "holy ground" of the inner city.

Tonight, a "completed" Jewish pastor takes turns with his Hispanic and Nigerian associate pastors as they minister to their new church members. Together, they share praise songs and Scripture readings as they stand in four feet of water in the Olympic-size swimming pool. The pastors wade from member to member as they listen to powerful testimonies: a college student has decided to take a bold Christian stand on the secular campus she attends; a former homeless man has traded his life and home on the streets for faith and his first apartment in five years; a 12-year-old boy decided to come tonight instead of running the 'hood with his "home boys."

As the pastors pray for their unlikely church members and baptize them in the name of the Father, Son and Holy Spirit, unexpected sounds echo off the blue cement walls. People are crying, applauding and laughing at the extraordinary sight of watching old lives become new. The worship band at the edge of the pool strikes up another song about giving glory to God and the baptism celebration-turned-swimming party continues into the night.

An Extraordinary Congregation

The baptisms at the Y are ordinary events for what many residents in Colorado's capital call an extraordinary congregation. Church in the City is a young church; now in 1995 it is just four years old, located literally at an urban crossroad that intersects a public high school, a multicultural/multieconomic neighborhood and Denver's gay district. It sits in an old Safeway grocery-store building, just yards from the city's busiest, most transient street, Colfax Avenue—a street where homeless men, prostitutes and drug dealers are as common a sight as bicycling police officers and businessmen in three-piece suits.

On the same block as what church members call the "New *Safe-Way*" building, sits a park, a Japanese Sushi Bar, a health food store, the Urban League offices and a ski shop. No one, then, is really surprised when they enter the sanctuary of Church in the City to find diversity at every level. This is, after all, holy ground.

But even with the surrounding visual contrasts, I doubt visitors are entirely prepared as they come to Sunday-morning services here. Church in the City just isn't like many traditional American church bodies I know of who worship in primarily homogeneous congregations and neighborhoods.

Here, everyone who walks through the door is greeted with a warm "G'Mornin'! Welcome to Church in the City" by an animated black woman, ushered to their seats by a professional-looking, middle-aged Greek and called to worship by an athletic, soft-spoken Hispanic in jeans and a T-shirt. Across the ceiling, in the simple-but-huge sanctuary (it's hard to believe this room was once filled with aisles and aisles of grocery products), hang flags representing a multitude of countries, missionaries and weekly prayers for the nations.

Visitors are handed a bulletin full of announcements and a list of the many service opportunities that include ministry at homeless shelters, jail outreaches, children's tutoring, youth recreational leagues, Bible classes and small-group fellowships. The activities, the diversity and the commitment of the leaders and 500 members are clear indications to me that this is a church alive with hope and a church responding to its culture in nontraditional ways as it proclaims the gospel of Jesus Christ in the city.

A Church of Vision

The church's qualities define what I believe the Church of the twenty-first century will look like: one full of compassion, enthusiasm and vision for the community in which it lives. The leaders at Church in the City have responded to what I call the felt needs of the people around them. As they have become closer with their neighbors, they have had to get personally involved in their lives. As a result, they have come to recognize that the inner city is holy ground—that is, as their senior pastor put it, "It is the ground where God's heart beats loudly for the people."

Like Moses, these Denver leaders understand that holy ground is where God is already present; they are just following behind Him, participating in the work He's already doing. I believe that the Church must, in fact, be a presence of holy light in a dark world if it's going to proclaim the transforming knowledge of Jesus Christ.

Like the worship band at the baptism declared, Church in the City is one that exists "for the glory of the Lord." You can find the phrase written across the backboards on the basketball court outside. And because these pastors admit that their entire "existence is for the glory of God," the ground and streets and neighborhoods around them are, indeed, holy.

Concern for the Inner City

But heading an inner-city church is not exactly what pastors Michael and Brenda Walker, and Jude and Cindy Del Hierro had in mind some 10 years ago when they were attending a suburban nondenominational church known then as Vineyard Christian Fellowship of Denver (it has since changed its name to Crossroads Church of Denver). The four friends were involved in leading small fellowship groups and a singles ministry. Week after week, they listened to Pastor Tom Stipe teach from the Gospels about Jesus' heart for the poor, the outcasts and the fatherless. Soon, they felt a growing concern to respond in action to that message by caring for the growing homeless population in Denver's downtown. They discussed the idea with Stipe and Assistant Pastor Randy Phillips (who now directs the national men's ministry called "Promise Keepers") about starting a ministry in the streets. The pastors, of course, gave them their blessings.

The Walkers and the Del Hierros started, like many churches I've seen, by taking small steps. First, they handed out bologna sandwiches to the homeless men who lived under the bridges in Denver. Their next step was knocking on the doors of a variety of urban ministries, seeking opportunities where they could just come alongside to help and serve.

The suburban ministry team initially settled into a weekly outreach service with the Salvation Army Blake Street Survival Shelter, a shelter only for homeless men and perceived by many local residents to be one of the "toughest" in the area. Eventually, ongoing relationships were fostered with the workers and visitors at the Denver Rescue Mission, at a drug and alcohol rehabilitation center known as Step 13, and at the Salvation Army Survival Shelter. Each Friday night, the

> ## "WE WEREN'T READY TO JUMP INTO THE CITY FULL-TIME. WE TOOK GRADUAL STEPS AS WE GOT INVOLVED. IN THE PROCESS, GOD STARTED INFUSING HIS HEART INTO US FOR THE PEOPLE."

four, and a following of 20 or so singles and couples from their suburban church, set up the band, led worship songs, distributed cookies and socks, preached and prayed for the men at Blake Street.

As the couples obeyed God's leading to enter the city and to help support the work of these established urban ministries, they found, too, that their hearts were beginning to change. As Cindy recalls, "We weren't ready to jump into the city full-time. We took gradual steps as we got involved. In the process, God started infusing His heart into us for the people."

The more steps the couples took, the more they were able to develop friends and insights in their new ministry opportunities. True, no one had trained them for this, no classes nor seminars were available for this kind of work. They learned as they went along—on-the-job training at its best—and called themselves "just ordinary Christians wanting to serve." They learned that to work with the homeless, they had to be consistent. They had to love with toughness, pray with confidence and work with untiring faith to proclaim the good news of

Jesus Christ to those caught in the often frenzied existence of urban life. They had to realize that God's love for these men whose homes were the streets and His call for their lives to be holy was just as real as it was for everyone else. This work and message was simply something they had to share.

Tough Love

This message of love was precisely what one young black brother named Ronnie needed to hear. The group first met Ronnie at the Blake Street Shelter. Ronnie was trying to "do a drug deal" there as the team was trying to talk with him about Christ. Ronnie didn't want to listen. He knew this "church-stuff" already, had known about the Lord a long time ago, but painful circumstances with his family forced him to live a life on the streets.

Still, each Friday night, the young stocky, streetwise leader would show up at the service for a dose of praise songs, preaching, prayer and possible deals, fully expecting to counter the Christians' claims on God's acceptance of him. But the consistency and tough love he saw from the "Vineyard folks" softened him. Finally, one Friday night, he made the greatest deal he ever got: He confessed a renewed commitment to follow Christ.

Within a year, Ronnie was back at Blake Street—this time serving with Walker's group and speaking to the other men of how God's love had changed his life. Today, Ronnie is being raised up as a servant-leader with the people who dared to enter his troubled world of street life and drug wars. He is an example of what I think is one of the greatest fruits of a ministry: indigenous leadership.

God's Leading

Ronnie's life, and a score of other men's, was changed because of the vision of ordinary suburban Christians who dared to dream. As the group continued to visit the city each week, it didn't take long for that vision to become contagious. More and more people came from the Vineyard to help, while more and more men like Ronnie were starting to respond to their care. It was a slow, sometimes difficult, process. But through a variety of hard lessons, drunken encounters, compassionate visits and consistent prayers, the ministry began to grow. The four leaders, now joined by a core of other faithful workers, simply wanted to continue responding to "God's leading."

After five years of community dinners, prayer sessions and outreach services, the group of urban workers from the suburbs began to discuss the possibility of a church plant. Some of their homeless friends were getting saved but weren't feeling comfortable wearing their soiled street clothes as they attended Sunday morning worship services at prominent downtown churches. (The suburb where the Vineyard met was too far for them to go.) Like their leaders, all the workers who had committed themselves to work with the Walkers and the Del Hierros were starting to sense a stronger call to the city, recognizing that the urban fields were a ripe harvest of opportunity. City life was seeping into the souls of these suburban Christians and God's Word regarding racial reconciliation, social ministry and evangelism was taking on new meaning to them.

Each time they met, the group began studying and discussing Isaiah 58:6-12, a familiar passage to those of us who have long been concerned about the Christian's response to the poor.

"Is not this the kind of fasting I have chosen: to loose the chains of injustice and untie the cords of the yoke, to set the oppressed free and break every yoke? Is it not to share your food with the hungry and to provide the poor wanderer with shelter—when you see the naked, to clothe him, and not to turn away from your own flesh and blood? Then your light will break forth like the dawn, and your healing will quickly appear; then your righteousness will go before you, and the glory of the Lord will be your rear guard. Then you will call, and the Lord will answer; you will cry for help, and he will say: Here am I. If you do away with the yoke of oppression, with the pointing finger and malicious talk, and if you spend yourselves in behalf of the hungry and satisfy the needs of the oppressed, then your light will rise in the darkness, and your night will become like the noonday. The Lord will guide you always; he will satisfy your needs in a sun-scorched land and will strengthen your frame. You will be like a well-watered garden, like a spring whose waters never fail. Your people will rebuild the ancient ruins and will raise up the age-old foundations; you will be called Repairer of Broken Walls, Restorer of Streets with Dwellings."

The passage pierced the heart of this growing community of active Christians and eventually became the foundation for their corporate ministry, which is precisely what I believe God's Word should do. They asked God how they might "repair the broken walls" of the city, how they might help "restore the streets with dwellings." They knew they had to begin to do more than the evangelistic services they'd been conducting for six years now in the shelters. They sensed they had to respond in a real, tangible way as they sought "to spend themselves on behalf of the hungry and satisfy the needs of the oppressed." New believers needed to be discipled, families needed support and children needed direction.

The idea for a church plant became more realistic and, consequently, they became more responsive to the needs of their new "church members." But no one, especially the Walkers and Del Hierros, imagined their outreach efforts in the shelters would someday lead to the formation of a church. I know they only wanted to respond to the needs of the homeless and obey God's leading in the process.

God's Sense of Humor

The idea that Michael would someday pastor an urban church is proof of God's sense of humor. Raised Jewish by wealthy parents in Long Island, New York (he even had a maid), Michael's thoughts about Jesus were a lot like the attitudes of the street kids for whom he now has a heart: Jesus was just a curse word you said when you were angry. And Michael was angry often as a youth.

Michael's search for peace and contentment literally sent him around the world, experimenting with drugs, mystical religions and every imaginable job. Just after the Jesus Movement of the 1960s, Michael wound up in California, where some Christians invited him to a mansion in Hollywood. Always ready for a party, Michael accepted the invitation. There, he experienced the transforming power of God as he heard for the first time about the love of Jesus. His life was never again the same.

Years later, after much study and growth and a move back to New York, Michael's parents saw a change and a peace in their son they had not seen before. As a result, they, too, accepted the Christian faith. Michael then came to Denver for a career move and quickly discovered what is now called Crossroads Church. There, he met his future wife, Brenda, whose upbringing was as different from Michael's as the communities that surround the church they now pastor together. Raised in a poor Hispanic family by her single mother, Brenda lived in the governmental housing projects of west Denver. She met Jesus as a child when a Baptist church sent a bus to the projects every week for Sunday School. God became for her the Father she never knew.

Brenda and Michael married under a Jewish canopy at Crossroads. Perhaps their cross-cultural marriage alone uniquely qualifies them to serve as senior pastors at Church in the City. But it is their careful study of God's Word and the serious responsibility in which they approach their leadership roles that make them effective ministers. Members find their authentic personalities and willing spirits refreshing, an inspiring example to the variety of folks who are a part of this church community. Brenda heads the women's ministry, and Michael oversees the discipleship, education and youth ministries, but both recognize that their work is nothing without the ongoing grace and mercy of the God who changed their lives.

High School Sweethearts

The Walkers also are quick to recognize that any success they enjoy at the church would never have been accomplished without the prayerful support of their many friends, especially associate pastors Jude and Cindy Del Hierro. Both Denver natives, Jude and Cindy were high-school sweethearts living in a Hispanic neighborhood not far from where Brenda grew up. After some friends invited them to an evangelical church, the young couple discovered a personal relationship with Christ. Eventually, they, too, found their way to Crossroads Fellowship where they met Michael and Brenda. All of their married lives, Jude and Cindy have ministered in music and worship. Jude now oversees the worship bands and outreach ministries at Church in the City and Cindy helps Brenda with the women's ministry (and anything else the church needs done) while raising their three children and newborn grandson.

A Diverse Leadership Team

The other pastors at Church in the City provide what I believe is a strengthening balance in diverse leadership. Andy and Toni Boden work as volunteer assistant pastors. A white couple married for 11 years, they are veteran urban residents who oversee the small home-group fellowships from the church and provide teaching and spiritual support for the other pastors.

Assistant pastors, Ade and Adeola Ajala, a Nigerian couple, have worked in missions around the world for 10 years and have recently been hired to oversee youth discipleship, especially to those teenagers caught up in gang activities. Imagine the effect of this team of pastors: a Jew, a Hispanic, a white and two Africans! I believe their very presence working together is an exciting example of God's power in bringing about racial reconciliation.

Holy Turf

These diverse pastors are quick to respond to their daily tasks at the church, but they also don't mind remembering their history, the time when the doors finally opened for the current church home on November 10, 1991, in the New *Safe*-Way building. They were amazed to have acquired the land and empty building for their church. Several multimillion-dollar corporations had tried unsuccessfully to buy the property from the owners. They wouldn't budge. But the Christian workers had found favor with the owners because of their faithfulness in the city and so were given a 20-year lease.

The acquisition of the building, the specific location and the birth of the church were significant signs to the community that God was indeed planting a Church in the City. The leaders learned that not only had their new location been a highly sought-after retail corner, but it also sat safely in one of Denver's only neutral territories for urban gangs. This was nobody's turf. Now, they said, it would be holy turf, a place where both sinners and saints were welcome.

The Church's Anthem

The new site also took on musical significance for one of the church's worship leaders, Brad Richardson. He recorded the events that surrounded the church's history in the lyrics of a song the congregation now sings almost weekly. It reminds me of how the old Negro spirituals told the history of my people. Its poetic message reflects the heart and the mission of these urban Christians. It has become almost an anthem, a reminder of where God has called them:

Standing here before Your fire burning, I hear Your voice,
Here I am.
I have seen Your glory and I'm yearning to do Your will, Here I
am.
You are holy, I'm standing on Holy Ground.
You are holy, I'm standing on Holy Ground.
You have heard the heart cry of Your people, You will deliver,
You have redeemed.
You have gone before us and behind us, to acquire this promised
land.
You are holy, I'm standing on Holy Ground.
You are holy, I'm standing on Holy Ground.

Becoming Urbanites

At the same time as the church "acquired this promised land," the pastors and core leaders were sensing a greater conviction that they could no longer leave their ministries in the city; they were to relocate by making their home in the community as well.

THESE FAMILIES RECOGNIZED THAT TO

BEST CHANGE A COMMUNITY FOR CHRIST, THEY

HAD TO BE *IN* THE COMMUNITY. I KNOW THAT

AS GOD SENT HIS SON INTO THE WORLD TO

BECOME A MAN, SO THE SAME GOD SENT

THESE CHRISTIANS INTO THE CITY TO

BECOME NEIGHBORS.

Within a year of their inaugural service, more than 10 families had relocated from their western suburb to the holy ground of their new urban neighborhood, just a few miles from the church. Because of their burden to minister in the city, they became convinced that they had to take on the attributes of urban life. They were learning in a real, experiential way the power of the Incarnation. They recognized that to best change a community for Christ, they had to be *in* the community. I know that as God sent His Son into the world to become a man, so the same God sent these Christians into the city to become neighbors.

As a result, the pastors wrote the following explanation of their history in a brochure that is available for any visiting friend:

> *What began in 1985 as a weekly outreach service at the Salvation Army Survival Shelter has since grown to a variety of ministry opportunities through our church. The Lord made it clear to us then that we could no longer come into the city, minister to the hurting and then pack up and leave. We believe the Lord has made it clear that we are to unpack our bags and leave them unpacked. We are to stay in the city, and through Church in the City, we want to impact our families and our community for the Kingdom of God.*

Having a clear "vision to serve as a Mission Bridge between the city and local suburban churches by providing opportunities and training for evangelism, ministry with the poor, and praise in the streets," Church in the City has become a multiethnic/cross-cultural fellowship where new believers are able to grow in the knowledge and the ways of the kingdom of God and where maturing Christians receive Bible and discipleship training, encouragement and opportunities to serve.

Joining CCDA

Consequently, this congregation has found a home and a support system as a member of our national networking organization, the Christian Community Development Association (CCDA). The pastors quickly discovered that CCDA provides the training and common vision they hadn't received elsewhere. They chartered a bus with two other Denver CCDA churches in 1993 to travel together with 20 of their own members to Jackson, Mississippi, for our fifth-annual national conference. (Imagine a bus full of blacks, whites, Jews and Hispanics driving through the deep South!)

Church in the City now partners with a dozen parachurch ministries (many of whom are also CCDA members) for special ministry events, such as a Christmas toy store, a score of interdenominational suburban churches that help out at neighborhood block parties, and a

core of other urban congregations who gather for monthly racial reconciliation services at the church and at youth programs.

A Model Church for the City

What does all this mean? It means that baptisms at the YMCA are as
common as free car washes where members "just want to serve" the
passing motorists who drive by. It means teams of ordinary Christians
share the gospel each week with the transient folks who frequent
Colfax Avenue. It means that professional athletes mentor public high
school students in the church's youth drop-in center. It means a variety of professional businesspeople help neighborhood children with
their homework in after-school tutoring programs. It means that
church members and musicians sing together in malls, jails and AIDS
hospices of the good news of Jesus Christ.

And, of course, it means that a lot of homeless friends are still visited at the Denver Rescue Mission and the Salvation Army Shelter.
That's where this exciting work all began.

As I see it, Church in the City is a model of what ordinary suburban Christians can do as they pray together and respond to the diverse
needs of their urban neighbors. I believe this is what the church of the
future should look like; one, in fact, not very different from the church
of the past—that is, the church of Acts. The church's attitude is one of
simple humility and genuine willingness to serve and honor Jesus
Christ in its members' daily lives. It's not always easy. But as Pastor
Michael put it, "We just want to see God getting glory for the work
that we get to be a part of. What we're watching is His transforming
love as we go from trash to treasure." Holy ground, to be sure.

=============Taking It to the Streets==============

*Regardless of what some people might think, suburban Christians have
an important role to play in bringing salvation to the cities. In this case,
it meant that these suburban Christians cared so much for their urban
friends that they relocated in the name of Christ to be among them. It
also meant establishing a supportive Christian environment called
Church in the City. As a natural by-product of urban life, this church
has become a powerful example of racial unity and Christian love.*

But it didn't happen overnight. These brothers and sisters took small steps during several years to establish relationships with urban folks while building ministry opportunities in the city. Having no books or ministry models to teach them, they literally learned as they went along, relying on God to reveal His plan to them through their corporate prayer and worship times. In the process, they experienced both unity and clarity of vision. Now, seeing people from all walks of life attending and a pastoral staff reflecting that diversity, I believe Church in the City represents the kind of congregation from which we can all learn what happens when people develop simple obedience and have willing spirits.

What kinds of small steps could you begin to take to bring God's love to the city where you live? Are you called to relocate, to live among the people others have overlooked? How could you begin to pursue that relocated lifestyle?

I pray that you will know the depths of the incarnation of Jesus Christ, a love so great that He chose to live and die among us while we were yet sinners.

The Real Graceland

In the heart of a typical Southern city, one megachurch has relocated to the urban crossroads, bringing with it a presence that provides grace, physical provision and vision. Just by being here, Mississippi Boulevard Christian Church is having a big influence in an old neighborhood as it is "Claiming the City for Christ."

The Saturday Minimall

On a hot, August morning in downtown Memphis, Tennessee, 50 or so businessmen and women are setting up shop in the shadow of Mississippi Boulevard Christian Church. They gather in the huge parking lot with their portable booths, boxes and chairs to sell everything from Afrocentric clothing and original crafts to toys and lawn-care services. While drinking orange juice and coffee, they exchange stories with one another about how their business started or what they hope to earn from today's "Saturday Minimall."

Across from their outdoor market, a circuslike tent is erected and nurses, interns and doctors from nearby hospitals are hurrying about inside it. Educational posters and medical instruments sit on the long tables as a large HEALTH FAIR banner hangs above them. Before long, couples, children and elderly friends begin to stroll through the busy parking lot. Some chat with the entrepreneurs, others get their blood pressure tested, and children chase balloons and smell the aromas of popcorn and hot dogs. A tall, well-dressed fortysomething man greets each person he passes with smiles, handshakes and a warm "Good to see you here!" No, he is not running for office; he is Pastor Alvin Jackson, senior pastor of the 7,500-member urban church sponsoring this summer festival.

The next Saturday, the same vendors and physicians come again to the parking lot at Mississippi Boulevard Christian Church. Hundreds of local residents and church members join them as they buy goods and receive medical care. This Saturday, they also cheer on athletes at the end of a six-kilometer charity run designed to raise money for a special housing project known throughout Memphis as the "Nehemiah Project."

For the next two August Saturdays, business cards will be exchanged, health awareness enhanced, products marketed and friendships born. More than 1,000 people from throughout the surrounding inner-city community will have walked through the parking-lot-turned-minimall. And by Christmas, 105 business owners and entrepreneurs will have gathered again, this time indoors in the multi-purpose hall of the church basement for a Trade Expo.

"Claim Our City for Christ"

Pastor Jackson and his 125 full- and part-time staff members believe the Expo and the minimalls are God's idea. They are well aware that divine inspiration is indeed required for them to reach the city best known for its barbecues, its blues and its king of rock and roll, Elvis Presley. The city of Memphis, along with the singer's shrine known as "Graceland," attract thousands of tourists and fans each year. But Mississippi Boulevard Christian Church doesn't mind the numbers; it is used to them. If anything, the additional people just give members another opportunity for creative outreach.

Let me point out, though, that a Southern city such as Memphis is not just known for its ribs and rock and roll history. It is often recognized for its polarized communities, both racially and economically; this is, after all, the city where our great leader, Dr. Martin Luther King Jr., was shot and killed just days after he had given his famous "I've Been to the Mountaintop" sermon.

I believe such intense polarization, then, forces God's people to seek innovative ways to transcend cultural and class barriers to reach their neighbors with the gospel. That's why I am so encouraged by what my brothers and sisters at Mississippi Boulevard Christian Church are doing to "Claim Our City for Christ," as their motto reads. They see the business ventures, their dozens of other holistic, creative ministries and their strategic location in the heart of the city as unique opportunities to bring people together while simultaneously supporting economic development—principles I've advocated for years.

The numbers alone show that such creative trade festivals have been successful for my friends at Mississippi Boulevard. The idea came when the pastor and some of his staff members were meeting for breakfast. "We'd been talking about how the church could help in economic development and someone had this grand vision for a festival. We tried it and it worked," recalls Pastor Jackson.

And though many residents come to the Expos simply for the marketing exposure, they leave with much more. "Even if I don't sell a thing," said one young store owner, "I've gotten to know some new friends in the business community."

As a result, several of these entrepreneurs have become members of

"NO CREED BUT CHRIST, NO BOOK BUT THE BIBLE, NO LAW BUT LOVE, NO NAME BUT THE DIVINE. IN ESSENTIALS UNITY, IN OPINIONS LIBERTY, IN ALL THINGS CHARITY."

the large congregation of Mississippi Boulevard Christian Church, a congregation that has relocated to the heart of Memphis's inner city and now sits at 70 North Bellevue Avenue. I believe one of the many strengths of this congregation is that it is willing to risk and try new things to reach the people.

Considering their many partnering efforts in ministries, such as the minimalls, Expos, citywide reconciliation services, housing projects, food services, educational and nationally known music programs, a fully equipped Family Life Center and the many tourists who come through their city each year, these folks are used to big crowds. But they know that each special ministry and their very presence in this neighborhood provide many more tangible symbols of grace than anything Elvis ever could. Cab drivers here will tell tourists that Mississippi Boulevard Christian Church is just as well known around town as the other Graceland. And for good reason.

"Freedom and Diversity"

Since the church first formed in 1921 as one of the few black congregations within the predominantly white, Christian Church (Disciples of Christ) denomination, Mississippi Boulevard Christian Church has always been active in the community. Its leaders and members have consistently supported the denomination's mandate to "stress freedom and diversity...energetic social activism and deep personal devotion."

They have supported missions in almost every part of the world, been committed to local development and community evangelism and have joined the other 4,200 North American congregations for annual strategic conferences and fellowship. They have helped send students from Mississippi Boulevard to the denomination's seminaries and colleges. In every aspect of their church lives, they have tried to remain faithful to denominational slogans such as "No creed but Christ, no book but the Bible, no law but love, no name but the divine" and "In essentials unity, in opinions liberty, in all things charity."

"For Such a Time as This"

When Pastor Jackson, a native of my great home state, Mississippi, and his wife, Tina, arrived at the church in 1979, he was able to build on an already well-established foundation that included an active membership of 400. Though he sees himself as "a quiet introvert who is much more comfortable at home reading," he knows this is the place and the job to which God has called him. As he puts it, "Getting up in front of seven thousand people each week [to preach] has to be the Lord because it's just not in me to do."

No doubt, Pastor Jackson's upbringing helped prepare him for his present position as well. His parents were committed members in the Disciples of Christ church in Indianola, Mississippi, where he was active in youth camps and Sunday School. (He grew up listening to me on the radio!) Young Alvin then went on to attend the denomination's Chapman College in California and later went to Duke University Seminary where he received his master's degree of divinity. I believe God used both his training and his family in preparing him "for such a time as this": to be the pastor of what has become the denomination's largest congregation in the world, black or white.

Just weeks after his arrival in June, 1979, Pastor Jackson started a radio ministry and initiated new services. When his feet were barely wet, a devastating fire broke out at the church, destroying its educational building and heavily damaging the sanctuary on Mississippi Boulevard.

"I hadn't meant to literally set the place on fire when I arrived. But it was a blessing in disguise because so many people got involved," smiles Pastor Jackson. Rather than wallowing in the loss, the pastor and his congregation immediately went to work on a new building program called "Project: Resurrection." While repairs were underway, the congregation met in a Seventh-day Adventist church. Within a year, however, the sanctuary was restored along with a brand-new educational building, and the church was able to move back to its original home.

Changing Facilities

But, as Pastor Jackson puts it, "Just as we were patting ourselves on the back and getting comfortable with what we had done, we looked around and discovered that we had outgrown the facility on Mississippi Boulevard." By 1984, the church moved its "Miracle on Mississippi Boulevard" and "Claimed Our Canaan" in a middle-class, multicultural suburb of Memphis known as Whitehaven, where it acquired 14 acres of land in addition to its new facility on East Raines Road. There, it enjoyed eight years of continued growth in both ministries and members. So much growth, in fact, that it once again had to look for a new facility.

The pastor and his team discussed the idea of building a new campus from the ground up but weren't sure this was the best use of their money. They decided to wait and see how God might direct them, making the most of their present but crowded situation.

Meanwhile, in downtown Memphis, a white Southern Baptist megachurch on Bellevue Avenue was outgrowing its facility in its changing urban community and was looking to move outside of the city limits. After building a massive campus in east Memphis, they moved their congregation to the new facility, leaving the old one empty for the next three years. Three times, Realtors approached the leaders at Mississippi Boulevard Christian Church in Whitehaven about buying the old Baptist church; three times they told Realtors the price was too expensive for their church budget.

Finally, Pastor Jackson and his staff decided it couldn't hurt to tour the 20-acre former Baptist facility. They were surprised by what they saw: a 3,200-seat sanctuary, 19 large assembly rooms, 221 classrooms, 44 offices, three 250-seat auditoriums, a library, a recreational center with an 8-lane bowling alley and a full-size, fully equipped gym. Because of both the size and the location of the old Baptist campus, the leaders decided to make an offer for one-tenth of the market price. To their surprise again, the owners accepted and by 1992, Mississippi Boulevard Christian Church had moved once again, this time back into the heart of the city in a facility that would allow it to grow and to influence the community in ways the members never before imagined.

A Bridge-Building Church

"We see ourselves as a bridge-building church. Consequently, we think the Lord has strategically placed us here," says the senior pastor. Bridge building, then, takes place in every facet of this church's active life. The average age of the congregation is 35, and people come from all economic and cultural backgrounds from throughout the city to attend one of several services, classes, or outreach or ministry events offered throughout the week at the transplanted church.

For instance, every Wednesday for lunch, the pastor invites friends from the local medical community, as well as the neighborhood, for a midweek lunch service. Some 600 professionals attend to hear Pastor Jackson teach from God's Word.

Led by Minister Leo Davis, the 170-member nationally acclaimed choir (70 percent of the members read music and there is a waiting list just to get in) often performs with the Memphis symphony for special holidays and events such as Dr. Martin Luther King's birthday. They also travel throughout the country performing at churches such as the Crystal Cathedral in California.

Life Focus '93

Another bridge-building effort has been the church's longtime commitment as part of an ecumenical interfaith group comprised of 40 diverse, liberal churches working together, to help meet some of the social needs in Shelby County. And in 1993, Mississippi Boulevard took the risk of being misunderstood (by some of its Shelby County friends) to support some staunch white conservative churches by helping spearhead a city-wide Christian unity conference called "Life Focus '93."

The event was held at the city's famous Pyramid sports arena and included participation from 50 evangelical black and white churches from all denominations (including the Southern Baptist church whose building Mississippi Boulevard now occupies). Life Focus '93 drew more than 20,000 people for a special racial reconciliation event, and the guest evangelists were John Guest and Tom Benjamin. Plans are underway for future similar conferences.

The purpose for the church's "risky" involvement? "We thought it would be for the betterment of the community," says Pastor Jackson. The result? Local residents and officials have been both kind and supportive of the works of the church, seeing Mississippi Boulevard as a positive resource center. The church has gained a credibility throughout Memphis for promoting economic justice and racial unity.

Calming Tensions

For instance, when two black youths were recently shot by white police officers, an incident that obviously created quite a bit of tension in the Southern community, leaders at Mississippi Boulevard were called on to help. They met with a number of other pastors to talk about what their role might be in calming the communities. The group of leaders encouraged the police to do cultural sensitivity training and to examine the extensive use of weapons on the police force.

"Usually when something like this happens in Memphis, people come here looking for leadership to help," says one member of Mississippi Boulevard. "The church has the credibility because we've been here, and have been involved in a number of battles in the community, working with both black and white communities."

And I believe by choosing to relocate to this community, the church has been able to build positive relationships with both communities and, in the process, has built a trust factor crucial for God's people as it goes about its Father's business.

The Nehemiah Project

Building bridges and bettering the community are what this church is all about. One special cooperative housing effort called the "Nehemiah Project" is proof. From its inner-city church home, Mississippi Boulevard Christian Church has joined the Shelby County Interfaith Ministries (comprised of 52 interdenominational churches) and the city of Memphis to help build 10 controlled, residential housing developments for working, low-income, first-time homeowners.

The concept of the Nehemiah Project was first developed and initiated by Pastor Johnny Youngblood of St. Paul's Community Baptist Church in Bronx, New York, and seeks to involve local churches to work cooperatively in reclaiming their community for Christ by addressing the whole needs of their neighbors. Youngblood's experiment was also tried in Baltimore and now a decade later, residents of those neighborhoods in both cities boast of comfortable homes at reasonable cost, two new schools and low crime rates.

The Memphis model hopes for the same success. Having the goal of building 2,000 brand-new, three-bedroom homes by the year 2000 in 10 neighborhoods including 125 to 250 houses each, Mississippi Boulevard (who donated 27 acres in the Whitehaven area) is excited about the possibilities that come as it literally builds new communities. Initially, neighbors in the area were concerned that the new cooperative effort might bring down their property values. But they have commitments from the churches for a strict counseling program for the first-time homeowners, a public park and the city's new multimillion-dollar decision to provide the infrastructure, so residents came around and supported the idea.

Each church involved in the Nehemiah Project contributes funds and workers to the community, and would-be homeowners apply exclusively through the churches. The program allows working folks who otherwise wouldn't be able to own homes the opportunity to do just that while simultaneously building relationships with church members. Consequently, the Nehemiah Project gives additional serving opportunities to church members as they work directly with homeowners in areas such as counseling or construction.

Longtime Memphis resident Barbara Guyton couldn't be happier about the Nehemiah Project. She will be one of the first homeowners and has since joined Mississippi Boulevard Christian Church along with her three children because of her involvement with the Nehemiah Project. Guyton has always worked hard as a housekeeper to support her children and has dreamed of owning her own home all her life, but was never able to afford it. Until now. When she was accepted into the program, it opened up a whole new area for her, a means of fulfilling a lifelong dream. As a result, she is "just bubbling over with joy," and is now an active member of the church. Her teenagers caught her enthusiasm as well and they've been committed Sunday School members ever since. Guyton has also become involved in helping others qualify to become homeowners.

Other local residents are happy about the Memphis Nehemiah Project as well, watching the cooperative effort with respect and admiration. In an editorial, daily newspaper officials praised the project, saying, "To see these congregations working together toward a common goal that will benefit hundreds of Memphis families itself is inspirational. Stir in the expected participation of city government and private business and you get a near-perfect example of what communities need to be doing to solve their housing problems."

Mississippi Boulevard Christian Academy
In addition to building a new housing development, the church is also

busy building a community Christian school. Mississippi Boulevard Christian Academy was founded in 1987 as a preschool. As the student population increased, the program expanded to six grades, several classrooms and 40 staff members, including 20 certified teachers.

Today, 308 students attend all seven grades at the Academy and participate in events such as multicultural exchange days with local Jewish and Catholic schools, field trips to the National Civil Rights Museum, concerts and art classes, in addition to their daily Bible studies. The curriculum focuses on a holistic approach to learning by encouraging students to develop spiritually, physically, socially, emotionally and cognitively, while actively responding to the needs of family and community. In recognizing individual differences, the school brochure reads, Mississippi Boulevard Christian Academy "fosters a zeal for learning and equips students to function effectively in a complex, technological and multicultural society."

"CHILDREN ARE MY PASSION. MAKING SURE THEY GET A GOOD CHRISTIAN EDUCATION, FOR ME, IS LIKE DYING AND GOING TO HEAVEN WITHOUT DYING."

Principal Tina Jackson (Pastor Jackson's wife) started out three years ago as the interim principal and just has not been able to leave. As a longtime public high school teacher with a master's degree in education, she remains a public school proponent. But she has to admit, she loves the freedom of being at the Christian Academy. "Children are my passion. Making sure they get a good Christian education, for me, is like dying and going to heaven without dying," she laughs. Though most of the students come from working, middle-class parents, Mrs. Jackson hopes to see the school grow more in outreach to the local neighborhood by providing scholarships for low-income parents, especially in an adjacent Asian housing project.

How is it being both a pastor's wife and a principal? "A joy! I was raised in the Southern Baptist church and so have been in church all my life. I love people," Mrs. Jackson exclaims. "Though it's a challenge to balance my responsibilities, plus being a mother to Cullen, our teenage son, I love being here. My husband never puts pressure on me and I always try to support his vision of building bridges in the community."

Manna Food Center

Across the multipurpose parking lot from the Academy is the Manna Food Center, another tangible sign of grace and bridge-building. On the wall of the small building is a colorful mural of Jesus feeding the 5,000. But the faces of those He feeds are local residents and church members, including Pastor and Mrs. Jackson. Inside, more than 150 volunteers toss canned beans and soup to each other as they prepare food baskets for their weekly deliveries to elderly friends on fixed incomes.

Each month, hundreds of families and friends are helped with groceries and encouragement through the food program. The outreach ministry also sends out teams to local homeless shelters, jails and prisons as ambassadors for Christ, "as though God were making his appeal through us" (2 Cor. 5:20).

Family Life Center

The church also views its Family Life Center as a wonderful way to reach the community. Says facilities manager and longtime church member, Andre Williams, "We have everything here to keep kids in church and off the streets." Having 14 youth basketball teams, 8 volleyball teams, karate classes, roller skating, a weight room, a bowling alley and handball courts, the busy youth-ministry workers make sure their teens don't have time to get bored. A clothing pantry, Christian bookstore, job placement program, women's center and counseling services all are additional signs that this church has something for everyone, inviting every person to come and fellowship there.

Jackie McHenry can attest to that hospitality. A native of New York and a Howard University graduate, Jackie came to Memphis after a debilitating illness and a painful divorce forced her to resign from her lucrative nursing position. Her parents were in Memphis so she thought she would bring her daughter for a short visit. That was three years ago. Since then, Jackie has recovered from both setbacks, thanks in large part to the friends she has made while volunteering at the Manna Center at Mississippi Boulevard.

When Jackie moved into her new home not far from the church, church members brought her tables, plants, pots and chairs for her housewarming party. Jackie continues to serve faithfully each week at the shelter, jail and Center, in addition to helping with the youth group and working part-time in the church accounting department. She's quick to point out that though much work remains to reach the community, this is "a church where God's work is going to get done. We're blessed to render the kinds of services we do here. Really, these are some of the greatest, most educated people I've seen. They are regular Southern country folks with Southern hospitality, but most of them have master's degrees or Ph.D.s."

The Church's Great Commitment

Pastor Jackson says his congregation at Mississippi Boulevard Christian Church is just trying to make an impact on its community and city by daring to build bridges and by trying new things. "The church must be willing to take some risks, be willing to be misunderstood and to make mistakes. This type of work doesn't come overnight; it takes a lot of time and trust," says the senior pastor. "What I tell our people is that a great commitment to the Great Commandment and the Great Commission will grow a great church. That's what we're trying to do here."

As a result, a faith community with a strong Christian presence that speaks to the whole person is showing residents here that there's a new and better Graceland in Memphis. One that, in the spirit of our own great Dr. Martin Luther King Jr., honors the King of kings instead of the king of rock music.

Taking It to the Streets

Think of all the wonderful ironies of this story: A large black Southern church moved from the suburbs into the city and into an incredible facility that a white church had built but abandoned for the suburbs. Mississippi Boulevard Christian Church (which is nowhere near Mississippi Boulevard) works with both poor Asian neighbors and wealthy government officials; its choir performs with the Memphis Symphony while its members minister to prisoners in jail; its leaders partner with other leaders who are both white and black, Protestant and Catholic, evangelical and ecumenical in order to provide comprehensive, holistic ministry to all its needy neighbors.

Although nothing about Mississippi Boulevard Christian Church sounds very ordinary, everything about it can be modeled. These brothers and sisters have simply asked God to lead them in meeting the felt needs of their community and city for Christ. What happened in the process was a powerful relocation of resources and role models. Yes, they have been creative and diligent in their numerous ministries, especially with their minimalls and housing efforts such as the Nehemiah Project. But the same direction and inspiration they have received from our creative God is available to us all.

What creative ministries could your church or ministry do to bring people and businesses together while sharing the gospel? How could you be a part of building bridges between all kinds of God's people in your city?

I pray that God will inspire you with innovative methods of reaching all people in your city with the good news of Christ, and that you will be courageous enough to follow wherever He leads you.

Building Hope on Sand

*In a historically black neighborhood called Sandtown in
Baltimore, Maryland, a core of white, committed Christians
relocated. Not only were their lives changed in the process,
but also a deep sense of community was formed and called
New Song Community Church, bringing new hope and life
to a neighborhood long believed to be dying.*

The Good News of New Song

I have said for many years that we cannot expect the government to
do those things God has called the Church to do. We know that in
many of our urban communities across the country, people are without adequate, decent housing. Barely enough decent paying jobs are
available to support their families, and worse still, a debilitating hopelessness hovers over these neighborhoods, like the thugs who deal
dope on street corners. We know that justice cannot come from government welfare programs alone, for they victimize the very people
they were designed to help; though well-intentioned, they are not
working. A quick glance into the streets might make some folks feel
discouraged.

But, thankfully, we have also seen that some of God's people are
finding wonderful solutions to the problems in our cities. A long
thoughtful look at one neighborhood in particular, in West Baltimore,
Maryland, is enough to make the biggest cynic shout for joy. Because
of a small interracial church, the story taking place in this black, historic community known as Sandtown-Winchester is an exciting example of what can happen when God's people take it upon themselves to
tackle the problems of poverty and economic injustice. Not only is it
encouraging, it is also good news.

A Neighborhood Resident Becomes a Role Model

Just ask Torey Reynolds. She grew up in Sandtown. Torey, a 35-year-old mother of four, remembers when this neighborhood was cluttered with boarded up row homes and drug dealers on each corner. She has watched friends move out and move on to better things while the community deteriorated. In Torey's lifetime, the population of this 72-square-block residential area has plummeted from fifty thousand to only ten- to twelve-thousand people to become one of Baltimore's poorest neighborhoods.

Many politicians in the past have ignored Sandtown because they said the residents didn't vote. Unemployment runs close to 50 percent, infant mortality exceeds that of many developing nations and the median income is less than $8,500 a household. Consequently, Torey can recall a time not so long ago when she herself was on crack, welfare and her last rope. Many mornings, she wasn't sure how she was going to make it through that day. Sure, she wanted a different, better life for her children, but change seemed too hard, too uncertain. Mere survival was all Torey knew.

That is, until Torey stopped in and met some friends at New Song Community Church. Torey had passed the three-story, renovated building at Gilmor and Presstman Streets in Sandtown many times before, wondering what it was all about, hoping someone there could help her and her family. But when she saw the work these Christians were doing in her neighborhood in the form of rehabilitated houses and resurrected hope, Torey knew she had come to the right place.

That was four years ago. Today, Torey Reynolds is an active member of the 125-member interracial Presbyterian church that began in 1988. She found a job as a community health-care worker through New Song's EDEN Jobs program, her children attend New Song's Learning Center and New Song Family Health Center when they are sick, and she is a proud first-time homeowner of one of almost 60 row homes rehabilitated through New Song's Sandtown Habitat for Humanity.

"People have seen a change in me. I was a drug user. I didn't know what I was going to do from day to day. Now they can use me as a role model. I've become a homeowner, a Christian person and employed," beams the tall attractive woman.

Torey never imagined she would ever own anything, let alone her own home. And she never thought she would find a position where she could help her husband support their family through a job she enjoys.

But, as she says, her dreams and her community have come alive, crime has decreased and her children have a brighter future because of the efforts of a group of diverse Christians at New Song Community Church, who are working together to better the place they call home. Let me point out, too, that New Song is not a megachurch or a mass organization with a megabudget. It is a small congregation of Christians who just happen to believe in a big God, and so it is making a monumental difference in its neighborhood.

When God's People Relocate

That's what happens when Christians relocate to troubled neighborhoods to incarnate God's love to the people there. Things begin to change in ways no government aid could ever provide. And when God's people relocate, not only are a variety of social needs addressed, but I believe reconciliation and unity in the Body are natural dividends of the process. The move also facilitates a variety of partnerships with other churches, residents and businesses.

What is happening in Sandtown is proof: More than 5,000 volunteers each year from countless churches and local organizations have come as partners alongside the residents to help renovate houses, provide health care or tutor children. Their combined efforts prove that neighbors can be empowered, and that a neighborhood can change itself not just because a few people decide to relocate, but also because God blesses the contributions each person brings to the work—contributions that are valued and esteemed by all involved.

Relocating to Sandtown

The strategy was not so clear, though, when in March 1986, New Song founders Allan and Susan Tibbels (along with their two young daughters, Jennifer and Jessica), Mark Gornik and a few other friends first started talking about relocating to the city.

After short-term work at our Voice of Calvary ministry in Jackson, Mississippi, Mark, a Baltimore, Maryland, native, completed his ministerial studies at Westminster Theological Seminary in Philadelphia, Pennsylvania, to become an ordained Presbyterian reverend. For years he had known the Tibbels, who were also from Baltimore; they had been his Sunday School teachers and the threesome had also worked in a campus youth ministry together. All three are white, grew up in the suburbs and yet have had a special place in their hearts for their urban neighbors and racial reconciliation. When I met them in the early 1980s, I challenged them to consider relocating to the city if they were really serious about these issues and about Christian community development.

■

"REPENTANCE INVOLVES 'OWNING' OUR

SIN, WHETHER ROOTED IN COMMISSION OR

OMISSION....REPENTANCE MEANS TURNING

FROM ONE WAY OF LIFE TO AN ALTERNATIVE

WAY. REPENTANCE IN THE BIBLE TOUCHES

EVERY AREA OF LIFE. IT IS AT ONCE SPIRITUAL,

SOCIAL AND ECONOMIC."

■

So after exploring several possible communities in urban Baltimore, the group decided by December 1986 to move into rental housing in Sandtown. A year later, they purchased homes and began renovating them as a team known unofficially as the New Song Fellowship. Because they loved the reformed theology of their Presbyterian Church of America denomination, they sought the blessing and support of their local presbytery. The regional denomination agreed to their request and plans were underway to build a ministry, and Mark was designated as the founding pastor.

The Great White Hope

For the first two years of their work, Mark, Allan and Susan didn't start any programs. They didn't become the Great White Hope by offering paternalistic help to their new neighbors. They didn't hand out gifts at Christmastime or turkey meals at Thanksgiving. Their only goal during those first few years in the community was to build relationships with their neighbors and to nurture friendships with the residents who knew Sandtown a lot better than they did.

As Mark puts it, "We came here out of repentance, to learn from our neighbors and just to be a part of the community."

Why? Because, as the Presbyterian reverend defines it, repentance is not feeling guilty or merely sorry; rather, "Repentance involves 'owning' our sin, whether rooted in commission or omission. Concretely, repentance means turning from one way of life to an alternative way. Repentance in the Bible touches every area of life. It is at once spiritual, social and economic. As white Christians, we believed it was vital that we turn from our complicity in a culture that is anti-black, anti-poor and anti-urban and turn to the biblical obligations of justice and reconciliation."

So Mark, Allan and Susan moved into the neighborhood many others had overlooked in order to seek reconciliation and justice. They joined the Sandtown-Winchester Improvement Association. They visited local churches, volunteered at the recreation center and talked to elderly residents who had raised their children there. All the while, they were renovating their new homes themselves out of their own pockets and had the help of only a few donations. Local residents weren't quite sure what to do with "these white folks" who had moved into their neighborhood. Some looked at them with skepticism, thinking they were either undercover narcotics cops or real estate moguls threatening to take over their historic community.

An Extra Challenge

Yet, Mark, Allan and Susan hung in there, though it was especially difficult for Susan (who would later become the tireless executive director of New Song's Learning Center). Only a few years before, Susan had endured an event that would change her family's life forever.

Allan had been playing basketball in a suburban church gym with several young people. As he went up for a layup, his feet got tangled and he smashed against the concrete wall. Allan broke his neck, leaving him permanently paralyzed and confined to a wheelchair. The accident also left him and his wife with a difficult but shared challenge.

How did Susan feel? "I learned that almost 90 percent of couples divorce after spinal cord injury. Being physically separated from Allan was my worst fear. I knew this was not something that happened to Allan. It was something God allowed to happen to us. I determined not to become one of the 90 percent. We would get through it together and find God's purpose."

For the next year, Susan helped Allan through the rehabilitation process, readjusted their lifestyle and had a wealth of friends and family support them through the experience. One friend quit her job to move in with the Tibbels and help care for the girls. Eventually, Allan's spirits came back and he returned to youth ministry at the church they were then attending. The family was recovering emotionally, but during the next four years, Allan continued to talk about a long-held commitment to racial reconciliation and social ministry.

So when Allan decided they should move to Baltimore's ghetto, Susan wasn't sure she could handle it on top of all they had just been through. "I didn't choose it (moving to Sandtown). It was Allan who felt called. But I believe God calls families, not individuals, so I just came along. 'Just coming along' meant moving from a five-bedroom, ranch-style home on 13 acres in suburban Baltimore, to a cold, dark shell of an inner-city row house."

After a few months in her new environment, Susan decided to stop being angry with "God and Allan for moving us to such difficult circumstances." Instead, she decided to try and find out why they were there. She says her attitude didn't change instantly but it was just the beginning of God's restoration work in her life. Now, as she daily interacts with children at the Learning Center and Allan directs the Habitat program, she can't imagine living or working anywhere else.

A New Vision Begins

As the relocated group prayed together and worked through their struggles, they eventually invited neighbors to join them. In the process, Sandtown's problems became their own. By 1988, they had begun "worship services" and Bible studies at Mark's house; they took children to the park, church camp and to the movies; and they continued to listen to their neighbors and dream together about how they could make their new home better for everyone.

Consequently, the residents started to respond, and as Mark puts it, "Given the historic and ongoing role of whites in oppressing our community, how we were treated is a testimony to Sandtown's capacity for graciousness."

If the reverse situation had happened, as it did about the same time New Song founders moved into Sandtown, the results would not be the same. For instance, a black family moved into an all-white neighborhood in South Baltimore. After being mistreated and forced to live under police protection, they finally gave up and moved away.

By November 11, 1990, along with new Sandtown friends, the founders moved worship services from Mark's living room into a renovated old convent that had been abandoned for 20 years and officially began New Song Community Church with the hopes of fulfilling my challenge to them and obeying God's call for their lives. Along with then-HUD Secretary Jack Kemp, U.S. Senators Dan Coats (Indiana) and Paul Sarbanes (Maryland), Baltimore Mayor Kurt Schmoke and more than 300 Sandtown residents and workers, I had the privilege of dedicating the new building with them.

As I spoke that day to the crowd about the three Rs (reconciliation, relocation and redistribution) of holistic Christian community development, I couldn't help but realize God was in our midst, pleased with the work of these brothers and sisters. Mr. Kemp also recognized that Sandtown's work symbolized "a new vision for our country, a new chapter in the civil rights revolution." No one could deny the purpose of this small congregation: To "reset the foundations of our community so that God's shalom—wholeness, justice, and joy—flourish." Today, in addition to the church, those foundations include a comprehensive health center, a job-placement program, multiple youth ministries and, of course, Habitat for Humanity.

Building on Hope

After renovating their new church building and their own homes, New Song leaders realized that housing for their neighbors was a major problem. They decided that one way they could demonstrate their Christian commitment to the community, then, was to begin a housing ministry through the church. That was just months after the new church opened. Because I believe owning a home is the first step toward the economic development of a community, it is exciting to see now the efforts of New Song Community Church in developing a vital work called Sandtown Habitat for Humanity.

Twelve full-time staff members and thousands of volunteers have literally transformed this impoverished area. Since Sandtown Habitat's offices opened in another renovated building (a 100-year-old carriage house), the focus area in the Sandtown-Winchester neighborhood has become a happy noisy place. Walk down the 1500 block of North Stricker Street and you'll hear hammers pounding, table saws screaming, lumber dropping and people laughing. Just about everywhere you pass on this block, the music of rehabilitation is playing and neighbors are chatting. Black and white residents, workers and friends are wearing T-shirts that say, "Building On Hope." What used to be a typical, abandoned urban area, complete with boarded-up homes and littered alleys, is today showing signs of resurrection.

And just dedicating a home becomes an incredibly symbolic event for the entire community. It communicates that housing is a great base from which to turn skills into assets, homes into a caring neighborhood and individuals into families. It reinforces a sense of belonging and personal space. It builds responsibility and dignity because it's a place they own. Dedicating a home in Sandtown is obviously about much more than just renovating houses; it's an event that depicts the very heartbeat of the holistic ministry of New Song Community Church.

No story better exemplifies this than the one Pastor Gornik recently told in *Urban Missions Journal*:

Very early Saturday morning on the day before Easter, Bubby Crosby awoke, tired and sore, but ready to begin the day's work. An assistant construction manager with Sandtown Habitat for Humanity, Bubby has spent the previous few nights on the floor of 1511 North Stricker Street, row house number 21 of 100 houses that Sandtown Habitat is rehabilitating in the neighborhood over the next few years. As each house nears completion, everyone is extra security-conscious, and Bubby's overnight presence ensured that no break-ins would tarnish this dedication day.

The staff and volunteers began to stream into 1511 North Stricker. From the neighborhood and across the Baltimore metropolitan area, black and white, affluent and poor, urban and suburban, came together around a shared commitment—the creation of decent and affordable housing for people in need.

Members of Epiphany Episcopal Church, the house sponsor and one of five Episcopal congregations laboring together on what has come to be known as "Episcopal Row," had provided the funding and volunteers. The homeowner contributed over 300 hours of "sweat equity."

Precious little time remains before the afternoon dedication, the culmination of seven months of hard work by hundreds of people. Activity is swirling. Every space of the house seems to have someone working on it. The sounds of hammers, saws, laughing and "dedication panic" fill the house as interior doors are hung, plumbing is finalized, the last pieces of carpet installed, and window shades are set in place. A house is being transformed into a beautiful home.

This house is for William and Mary Elliott, both in their sixties. Community residents for over forty-nine years, today they are saying goodbye to high rents and substandard housing. For the first time in their lives, they will own their home. Both are strong Christians. Mr. Elliott in particular will be bringing leadership skills to the block. As the first of twenty homes to be completely gutted and rebuilt on this block, this home's dedication is a great day for the neighborhood.

At 3:30, the sound of gospel singing replaces the hocking and plocking of hammers. Outside the house on the street, over 100 neighborhood residents, friends and Habitat homeowners have gathered to celebrate the dedication. It is time "to have church," time to celebrate the goodness of Jesus and acknowledge God as the builder (Psalm 127:1, Heb. 3:4).

Every house dedication is a living sermon, a tangible demonstration of God's love and power. Leading the service is LaVerne Cooper, Co-Executive Director of Sandtown Habitat, and she is particularly pleased this day. This house, which had been vacant for twenty years, had been her grandmother's home. In fact, this is LaVerne's old block; the vacant house next door was where she grew up. Now LaVerne, also a Habitat homeowner, is leading the way in rebuilding her former block.

Multiple components filled the vibrant dedication service. Special music was provided by the New Song Community Learning Center Choir. Keys and a Bible were presented to the new homeowners. Other Habitat families presented flowers. Testimonies were offered by the Elliotts, Epiphany volunteers and other community leaders. Linking the testimonies together was the realization that new relationships have been formed across immense racial, social and spatial chasms. A closing prayer and house blessing was pronounced.

Finally, the moment has come to cut the ribbon. Bubby, a lifetime resident of Sandtown, joins Mr. Elliott and members of Epiphany for the honors. To the sounds of cheers and clapping, the Elliotts enter 1511 North Stricker Street new homeowners. Life is affirmed; a community long put down is rising up.

And so an entire neighborhood has rallied together at the emergence of realized dreams. Lifelong resident and Pentecostal pastor Clyde Harris couldn't be happier about his neighborhood's new life. Known and respected as Elder Harris, this enthusiastic brother has committed his heart and soul to the community. As he has watched many ministries and organizations come and go, he has chosen to stay and raise his children there.

Either as a pastor, a worship leader for special events at New Song or now as a staff member with Habitat where he works with Family Nurture, Elder Harris has been a faithful, committed Sandtown champion. Now through Habitat, New Song and our national organization, the Christian Community Development Association (CCDA), he has a wider ministry. His grown daughter Shelly works part-time at the Learning Center. (CCDA folks will remember her as the woman who directed the New Song children's choir when they hosted our sixth-annual national conference in Baltimore, and her dad as the energetic singer on the worship team.)

New Song Learning Center

In addition to dedicating houses, New Song members such as Elder Harris are dedicated to building dreams in their young people by rallying behind them in a variety of programs. Multifaceted in nature, the New Song Learning Center opened its doors in 1991 to "enrich and develop the educational and leadership potential of children and youth in our community."

Like our work in Mississippi, the folks at New Song are investing in more than 100 neighborhood youth by providing everything from a cooperative preschool and an after-school program to summer camp and a scholarship fund for one major goal: to have their young people return to the community after they graduate from college.

Each aspect of New Song's facilities is carefully decorated and organized for the children and their families. Susan believes, "When they come here, to church or to visit the doctor in the health clinic, everything should be the best we can give them because it is done in the name of Jesus. The visual appeal is an important part of our philosophy to minister to the whole person." So from the first-rate classrooms of their newly formed middle school, New Song Academy, to the colorful banners that brighten the sanctuary of the church, everything about New Song communicates new hope and growth.

Two More Pastors Join the Staff

The leaders are no exception in communicating hope and growth. Three years ago, two more enthusiastic pastors, one white and one black, joined Mark on staff and moved their families into the neighborhood.

Pastor Steve Smallman leads worship for Sunday morning services, dedications and other weekly and major events and Pastor Wy Plummer (who plays the bass guitar and makes music with Steve) is executive director for EDEN Jobs started in 1994, where 50 job placements were made in the first year alone. Both new pastors are

▮

RELOCATION IS NOT A SACRIFICE....IT IS

THE BEGINNING OF GREAT JOY, PURPOSE

AND SPIRITUAL GROWTH. "COSTS" MAY BE

INVOLVED,...BUT THE GREATER COST WOULD

BE NOT TO SHARE IN A COMMUNITY OF NEED.

▮

thankful to be a part of building Sandtown back up and seeing their community grow. Pastor Smallman, though, confesses, "It's a special challenge for pastors here, especially in learning about our community and in knowing our neighbors. We're having our hearts broken over the same issues that break theirs. Really, I'm learning how to learn and to be a neighbor."

Not a Sacrifice

Pastor Gornik believes that the combination of the staff's relocated lifestyles and each distinct ministry, as well as the interracial congregation, have all served as a "great apologetic for the gospel to non-Christians throughout Baltimore. People are curious about us because relocation captures the imagination of the city. Really, though, it was more important for us to relocate than for our neighbors to have us here. We've gained great neighbors and a chance to live out our faith."

In short, this team believes that relocation is not a sacrifice. Instead, they see it as the beginning of great joy, purpose and spiritual growth. "Costs" may be involved, they say, but the greater cost would be not to share in a community of need.

"Any struggle we have pales in comparison with the daily life issues of many people in our neighborhood. It is a privilege to share in both the struggles and the joy of a community. Christians missing out on this are missing out on the front lines of God's urban agenda, the gospel of community and the Lord's reconciliation purposes," says Mark.

A Good Thing Happening

So New Song Community Church in Baltimore is about the business of bringing God's reconciling kingdom to a neighborhood that before had known much pain and abandonment. They are doing this, as their Sandtown Habitat motto reads, by "Building a Home, Loving a Family, Nurturing a Community."

I'm proud of the work my brothers and sisters have begun in Baltimore and that they have stayed committed to seeing it through. Their work is a testimony to the power of God's love demonstrated in the lives of His servants.

But perhaps Sandtown resident and homeowner Torey Reynolds said it best: "I think my community in the future will become more spiritual and people will believe in God because of New Song. This place was falling apart before New Song was started; now people are wanting to be a part of it because it's a good thing happening."

Taking It to the Streets

New Song Community Church is about many exciting things. Mostly, it is about the work of building God's kingdom by building houses, hope and vision in the lives of its neighbors in Sandtown. From housing renovation and job training to youth programs and worship services, all these wonderful things are happening because a group of Christians dared to relocate to the inner city, taking with them the Resurrection message of the gospel.

One distinguishing feature about New Song, though, is its deep sense of community. This is a group of Christians, white and black, who really like each other, who share the same passion of seeing their neighborhood transformed for Jesus Christ. I believe unity quite naturally occurs when God's people sincerely and humbly follow His leading by relocating among the poor. Consequently, the principles of repentance, reconciliation and incarnation take on new meaning for these believers as God uses each to reach the city. In its purest form, New Song Community Church means a new community is working together to bring a new hope to the place they call home.

How could you get involved in cooperative efforts to "resurrect" new life in the urban neighborhoods that surround you? In what ways could these new definitions of repentance and reconciliation motivate you in your own life?

I pray that you would be a part of God's reconciling work to bring justice and repentance to the city where you live.

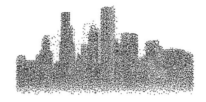

REDISTRIBUTION

*If anyone has material possessions and sees his brother
in need but has no pity on him, how can the love of
God be in him?*
—1 John 3:17

9

The Church Next Door

*Lake Avenue Congregational Church in Pasadena,
California, is a powerful example of what a large
predominantly white church strategically located can do
to offer resources and respect to their surrounding
neighbors in the name of Jesus.*

There's No Place Like Home

"There's no place like home." That's what Dorothy said in *The Wizard of Oz*, and I couldn't agree with her more. I would bet that most of us feel that way about the place where we grew up or the community where we now live. We all know it is a part of our human nature to have a sense of roots and family, a safe place we can go where we know people will love us, support us and encourage us to press on. Of course, there's no greater need for this kind of security than in our home churches.

That's exactly how I feel about Lake Avenue Congregational Church, my home church in Pasadena, California. When my wife, Vera Mae, and I moved back to California from Mississippi in 1982 with plans to retire, the pastors and members at the church reached out to us in ways that made us feel important to them and significant in their church. At the same time, I realized that though many white brothers from California had supported our ministry in Mississippi, I had not established the kind of deep friendship with them that was essential for our mutual growth. By coming to Lake Avenue Congregational Church, God gave me the opportunity to nurture such friendships.

The Priorities of the Gospel

Pastor Paul Cedar (now president of the Evangelical Free Church of America denomination) was the senior pastor when we started attending the church. He and I would meet often to discuss how we could work together to reach the changing Pasadena community with the good news of God's transforming love. He would ask me questions, pray for me and listen to me dream about how the Body of Christ could better reflect the Kingdom principles of justice and reconciliation. A special friendship formed between us, and I knew Paul would be as committed to me as I would be to him. We also knew that Lake Avenue could have a great influence in our surrounding community.

As Pasadena began to experience both an ethnic and economic transition, the kind so many other cities have gone through, the folks at Lake Avenue recognized that God had placed them strategically in this location at 393 North Lake Avenue. They had been there for almost 100 years. This was their home. Though they could have moved out of the city and into a less challenging, more comfortable suburban area as many large predominantly white churches have done, this church chose to stay put. This was, after all, a church that had long been committed to the priorities of the gospel.

A Rich Heritage of Evangelism

Lake Avenue enjoys an exciting history of reaching the world through its strong missionary program as well as its rich heritage of evangelism. In 1903, just seven years after the church was founded, Isaac Kuykendall was sent by one of Lake Avenue's adult Sunday School classes to China as the church's first missionary. Since then, our Sunday School and missions programs have planted more than 200 churches for 10,000 Christians in the Philippines, founded a seminary in Nigeria, built a Christian hospital in Bangkok, sent missionary pilots to New Guinea and Ethiopia, sent several college-age members to the very first Urbana Missions Conference and helped establish the U.S. Center for World Missions with Lake Avenue member Dr. Ralph Winter.

Today, the church has a million-dollar missions budget coming directly from the congregation, and supports 125 missionaries in 25 countries through dozens of missions agencies. The church has 4,000 church members, 25 percent of which are minorities, and our collective commitment for reaching the world, as well as our very presence here in the community, has been a sign of our stability. In our 100-year life, our church has only had four pastors! So when my family and I moved to Northwest Pasadena, a culturally diverse neighborhood a mile from Lake Avenue Congregational Church, I knew I had found a home.

Rebuilding the Community for Christ

I started attending the Sunday School class Dr. Peter Wagner was teaching. There, I met some other men who would become lifelong friends, friends for whom I am eternally grateful. As we settled into our new home and our new church, Vera Mae and I were quickly realizing that Pasadena was a city plagued with the same troubles as many others: gang violence, illiteracy, drug traffic and single-parent homes. Forget retirement in a nice, quiet neighborhood; we discovered that the heart of the "poor" section of Pasadena, the one we planned to move into, had one of the highest daytime crime rates in California.

We then learned that the corner of Howard and Navarro Streets was a center for all kinds of illicit activity, so I told my wife, "That's where we need to be." Shortly after we moved in, I started a Bible study and prayer group with people who shared my concern for the community and Vera Mae began a Good News Club for the children. We just knew we had to respond to our neighbors in some creative, effective ways to help rebuild the community for Christ.

"Let's Get Together and Push"

By 1983, we decided to form a local outreach center that would target urban youth and provide them with after-school tutoring, recreational activities, a camping program, a business club and, most importantly, Christian role models. We called it the Harambee Christian Family Center. (Harambee is a Swahili word that means "Let's get together and push.") During those early years, I remember asking God for people to help us as we started the Harambee Center. We knew we couldn't do it alone. Christians never can. That's why we need each other in the Body of Christ if we are ever going to change our cities with the good news.

So God sent us help through the support and care of new friends from our new home church of Lake Avenue Congregational Church. Specifically, He sent four white men to me who have been with me ever since: Roland Hinz, George Terzian, Steve Lazarian and Mark Bassett. We spent time together over breakfast, met often for prayer, and talked on the phone about lessons we were learning, visions we felt called to or problems we were confronting. We've all become good friends, and through the years, these men have supported me and our work in a variety of positive ways. We love each other.

But to be honest, my friendships with these godly men showed me much more than just mutual support; they proved to me that not all white folks are calloused to the needs of the inner city. Here, after all, was a group of Christians who were willing to put their money and their personal time where their mouths were by giving to us out of their love for Jesus Christ. They started volunteering at Harambee, organizing fund-raising events for us and recruiting other church members to help. These four men got so excited about the potential influence we could have together in the community that they began to develop a larger vision for the nation. As a result, they have been primarily responsible for my national ministry—the very backbone of it.

Because these men took our friendship and our work seriously, they were instrumental in our efforts to establish the Harambee Christian Family Center, the Christian Community Development Association and *Urban Family* magazine. And each man has continued to encourage and sustain us ever since. Roland, Steve and Mark are gifted and generous businessmen who have given literally thousands of dollars of their own money for our work, a work they identify with in deeply personal ways. George, a highly successful head-basketball coach at Pasadena City Community College, serves on our board of directors of the John Perkins Foundation, bringing with him a deep commitment to develop the leadership abilities of our young men. We work together so well that when we see a need, we respond as a team. For instance, when a homeless family was living in a tent behind our center, we helped them find housing. Then Steve and I helped form Pasadena's only family shelter, The Door of Hope.

The Harambee Christian Family Center's 1995 board of directors also show great dedication:

Mr. Stanley Lazarian, Mrs. Addie James, Mr. Bert Voorhees, Mrs. Claretta Smith, Mrs. Betty Jo Ford, Mr. Richard Culpepper, Mrs. Maxine Gebbie, Mrs. Dinah Roberts, Mr. Jim Wilson, Mrs. Susan Long, Mr. Marcus McDaniel, Mr. Rudy Carrasco, Mrs. Dorothy Ertel, Mr. Derek Perkins, Ms. Priscilla Perkins and Ms. Colleen Jamison.

Another person who has been influential at Harambee is Orel Hershiser, baseball player for the Los Angeles Dodgers. Orel has been expending his time and energy to help my daughter Priscilla (who will serve as principal) organize fund-raising dinners for Harambee's future elementary school.

Lake Avenue's Commitment to the Bible

All four men have been members at Lake Avenue Congregational Church for many years and reflect the vision of our church to influence the world and the community with the love of Jesus Christ. Walk into the sanctuary, and you will know this is a place that has always been a clear voice for sound biblical teaching. On the walls in the huge worship center hang beautiful red and blue banners that reflect our

■

IN A SOCIETY THAT HAS SO MANY DIVERSE

PHILOSOPHIES, RELATIVE TEACHINGS AND FEEL-

GOOD MESSAGES, IT IS REFRESHING TO SEE

SUCH A CONSISTENT DEVOTION TO THE TRUTH

AND TO THE ABSOLUTES OF GOD'S WORD.

■

Christian commitment and communicate reminders such as "We honor God in our personal lifestyle," "We glorify God in our worship," "We are ministers together," "We are empowered by the Holy Spirit" and "We are guided by God's word."

This encouraging commitment to the Bible was one quality that first drew me to Lake Avenue. In a society that has so many diverse philosophies, relative teachings and feel-good messages, it is refreshing to see such a consistent devotion to the truth and to the absolutes of God's Word. Ours is a church that has always been devoted to sound, exegetical Bible teaching. And I'm proud, too, that the staff and members of Lake Avenue Congregational Church have taken it upon themselves to become a multicultural congregation by fostering several ministries that reach more than 40 diverse ethnic groups represented in our community.

Friendship Corner Community Outreach Center

One such ministry the church started in 1984 is called the Friendship Corner Community Outreach Center. Located just a mile from Lake Avenue in a largely Hispanic community, this creative ministry meets in an old Quaker meeting house. Its primary focus is to reach the Latino families who live nearby with the gospel, because only 5 percent of Hispanics in the area attend any church at all.

Bilingual Center director and Lake Avenue staff member, Steve Klein, believes the Friendship Corner provides visible demonstrations of God's love because it meets people where their needs are. So with a soccer field in the backyard for the local kids and a big blue sign out in front that advertises in Spanish when medical help, English and sewing classes, food distribution, youth clubs and Bible studies are available here, the Friendship Corner is providing help and hope to the immigrants and neighbors who live next door.

Feron Dolce is particularly glad for the Friendship Corner. Five years ago, he had arrived alone in the United States from Haiti and had no plans and no people to call on for help. He wandered around the streets of Pasadena, homeless and hungry, until he walked right into the Friendship Corner.

Steve Klein welcomed Feron and asked how he could help. Feron was just looking for a job, he told Steve. He didn't want any handouts; he did, after all, have his pride. Steve had been wanting to hire someone to help clean the building once a week and so he offered Feron the job. Feron accepted.

Today, Feron credits the Friendship Corner as the "place where my life turned around." He met his Latino wife (who attends Lake Avenue) here, and now owns his own home, is fully employed and has renewed his commitment to Christ.

Preaching God's Word with Excellence

The Friendship Corner and other ministries like it reflect the kind of vision Lake Avenue Congregational leaders have always shared. When Pastor Cedar moved on to his new position in Minnesota, our congregation brought in a new senior pastor, Dr. Gordon Kirk, who arrived with his wife, Patricia, and two children, Kristina and Jonathon, in 1991.

Pastor Kirk has continued the tradition of strategizing how he can best lead his congregation in influencing the city as well as in preaching God's Word with excellence. He has shown passion, commitment and integrity in his leadership style and in his personal Christian witness in reaching out.

Pastor Kirk has also recognized, as he puts it, that in the "last 25 years, America has begun to see that missions can involve local communities. We have rich roots here that say we care about others. Our heritage has been good, and in the last few decades, Lake Avenue has been turning with the tide, not away from it, in realizing that Pasadena has a rich diversity of ethnicity."

Racial Reconciliation Issues Addressed

In the process, Pastor Kirk is not afraid to ask for help when it comes to the issues of racial reconciliation and Christian community development in our changing city. The Sunday morning after the April 1992 Los Angeles riots, for instance, Pastor Kirk asked me to preach to our congregation; he believed a black evangelist like me could provide insights into the urban tragedy he and his staff might not have considered. Then he appealed to the members to give a special financial offering (we raised $28,000 that Sunday) for outreach efforts in Los Angeles, and he formed teams to help distribute food, clothing, Bibles and hope to those victimized during the riots.

Soon after, six black boys were shot down on our streets, three of which were killed instantly. It put the city in an uproar and Pastor Kirk again came to me, asking me to put together a committee that looked like the community and could be involved in reaching our city with the peace and love of Jesus Christ. Pastor Kirk also asked Roger Bosch, Assistant Pastor of Missions, Evangelism and Community Outreach, to join me as together we helped form a task force committed to bringing about racial reconciliation in our community.

Of course, I was thrilled with the opportunity, knowing that our church had both the corporate resources and the personal commitment to build bridges between our culturally diverse neighbors and ethnic churches. I was also thrilled to work with Roger, a cross-cultural veteran who had been on staff with Campus Crusade for Christ, International in Germany for many years before coming with his family to Pasadena on furlough.

One of Roger's first jobs at the church when he came in 1992 was to organize international, evangelistic outreaches during the World Cup Soccer matches. Two hundred and twenty-seven new members were added to our church family and 73 people were baptized as a result of those outreaches. So I knew Roger would be a great man to work with in promoting the biblical mandate for racial reconciliation in our community.

Neighborhood Christian Partners

Roger quickly identified leaders from some of the 42 cultures within a five mile radius of our church. "The world is literally on our doorstep," he told me. "Though we feel like the novices in our changing community, we are exactly where God intended us to be. This is a strategic place."

Roger was right. As we worked together, a coalition of 30 churches and a mailing list of 60 people in Northwest Pasadena was formed, known as "Neighborhood Christian Partners." The task force at Lake Avenue met for months, though, before we fostered such partnerships. We understood that in Northwest Pasadena where there is poverty and racism, a big church such as ours (that literally takes up an entire block) could too easily overpower small black and Hispanic congregations.

We decided to organize neighborhood partnerships by building mutually supportive relationships with their leaders as we worked together with these churches. We made it clear that by focusing on our "Jerusalem" in Northwest Pasadena, we hoped to rally evangelical leaders to meet regularly through Neighborhood Christian Partners. To say the least, we have all benefited from the partnership.

Then we asked these Christian leaders, "How can we best have an impact on our community together?" They developed a variety of creative ideas. Cultural events were planned, pastors and choirs began to swap pulpits and some of our members attended other worship services. Our hope has been that Lake Avenue members would also become dual members with some of these smaller congregations and by doing so, provide some of the human power and resources necessary to help these churches while simultaneously learning about another culture. These members would then give their tithes to the partnering churches, help in their children's ministries and pray with their new friends.

We believed that by becoming partners, mutual relationships could be built, resources provided and we would not be patronizing. As Roger says, "Our work together is complementary so there isn't a feeling of competition. We want everyone at Lake Avenue to know what's going on in the community so we stress lifestyle Christianity. We realize we can't do everything, but through the partnerships, we know others who can."

And the partnerships are working. For example, one day a man dropped in at the Friendship Corner. He was a leader at a local Lutheran church and wanted to know if Lake Avenue Congregational had a bus his church could borrow for an evangelistic outreach they were planning for neighborhood children.

Because Steve Klein (the Friendship Corner director) had just attended a luncheon for Neighborhood Christian Partners, he told the leader, no, Lake Avenue didn't have a bus, but he knew of a church that did. Steve referred him to New Revelation Baptist Church and also told him that Lake Avenue had several bilingual members who could help in the outreach. So more than 100 children from the community were bused by New Revelation Baptist, and First Lutheran Church hosted its evangelistic party while several Lake Avenue Congregational members joined the ministry event. Not only were urban children introduced to the gospel that day, but the Body of Christ also came a little bit closer to unity.

Our partnership committee also formed a center for Spanish-speaking ministries. Already, Spanish- and Chinese-speaking congregations were meeting in our building as another way to reflect the community. Roger has also helped partner with other language-speaking churches by making resources available to them. He finds a "mutual encouragement with the pastors as I meet with them."

Two Fuller Theological Seminary students attending Lake Avenue who had a heart for the Hispanic community found out about the Hispanic church, became involved and started an after-school program at the Friendship Corner with first-generation Hispanic kids. One student leads a group of 6- to 12-year-olds, the other a group of 13- to 18-year-olds. Recently they also decided to meet for the first time with the kids' parents by inviting them to a potluck at the Center. Thirty-five moms and dads came and friendships were born that night.

Reaching Out

Because Pasadena is an international city that includes the arts, universities and seminaries nearby, Lake Avenue has also recognized the opportunity for making a world of difference right here in our own community. We have begun a variety of ministries in reaching out to international students at California Institute of Technology and Fuller Theological Seminary, often using English as a partnering tool for personal evangelism and discipleship.

Some of our church members invite international students to attend 1 of 30 adult Sunday School classes, or to join them for community service projects or small-group Bible studies that meet throughout the week. Some students also get involved in our specially designed class called "BodyLink," which focuses on tapping into people's gifts and immediately getting them involved in ministry.

▌

"WE ARE A CHURCH IN PROCESS, NOT RAISED

UP TO THE MODEL. WE ARE ON A LEARNING

CURVE....WE SEE OURSELVES AS MEMBERS OF

THE KINGDOM RATHER THAN MEMBERS OF AN

EXCLUSIVE CHURCH."

▌

At least 2,000 of our members are plugged into small groups of some sort because, as Pastor Kirk says, "One of our goals is to develop small groups all over this valley. So we're trying to start with smallness. I'd rather be known for our caring and people contact than for our facilities or location."

Another way Lake Avenue reflects concern is by hosting special dinners for the business community. Because many of our members are businessmen and women, they will host monthly dinners for colleagues and other business leaders. They invite a Christian speaker who is also an expert in the group's field of business to address the dinner group.

An average of 125 people attend these business outreach dinners, where over half indicate an interest in Christianity. Pastor Kirk believes this is an influential way to reach the community while simultaneously building up the resources of the church.

A Church in Process

What really distinguishes Lake Avenue Congregational Church is that while it has maintained its focus on creatively reaching the community, it has been realistic in its identity and mission for God's kingdom.

As Roger Bosch puts it, "We are a church in process, not raised up to the model. We are on a learning curve. We're trying to be who we are and if a person would fit better somewhere else, we try to encourage him to be where he can best be ministered to. We see ourselves as members of the Kingdom rather than members of an exclusive church. We would rather see personal growth take place with the unchurched. That's what we feel called to, to reach or to make resources available to our neighbors for Christ."

And so my home church has deepened its commitment to influence a changing community by choosing to change with it, yet without compromising its values. My brothers and sisters here know that as we try to reach the whole community, a community that is whole will be raised up.

With strong efforts to redistribute our talents and resources and to reconcile ourselves to one another, that is, as Pastor Kirk defines it, to reestablish a God-intended and God-given relationship, Lake Avenue Congregational Church in Pasadena is challenging its members not just to send money to the mission fields throughout the world, but also to get personally involved in the mission field that's right next door. We know we have a long way to go, but with the support and security of a strong home church, there's no place else we'd rather be.

Taking It to the Streets

I love my home church, Lake Avenue Congregational Church, and I know people here love me and my family. I've seen that love demonstrated countless times in their personal and corporate commitment to take the whole gospel to the whole world. They are sincerely concerned about how they can become better neighbors to the changing Pasadena community. Consequently, they have begun to explore a wonderful variety of options for what role they might play in Christian community development.

From its partnerships with local churches and its world missions program to its Friendship Corner and sound commitment to teaching God's Word, Lake Avenue models an exciting church in process, growing in both its understanding and its responsibility as a Christian steward in the city. The pastors, staff and members here know that because they have been given much, much is required of them. So they are always praying for and seeking opportunities to serve God in their respective callings.

What resources does your church have that can contribute to developing Christian community? How could you help organize a partnership with local churches to better reach your community for Christ?

I pray that your home church provides the love, support and vision for you as mine has for me, as together we help build God's kingdom on earth.

From Riots to Renaissance

West Angeles Church of God in Christ is the largest congregation within its denomination. And for good reason. It has the resources, the integrity and the rich blessings of God to transform its surrounding city of Los Angeles in a variety of ways with the love of Jesus Christ.

An Icy Beginning

On January 8, 1969, a tall, stately, 29-year-old pastor walked into an ice-cold sanctuary in South Central Los Angeles. The 50 or so Church of God in Christ members waiting inside were hardly warm and inviting. They had been feuding with the young pastor's bishop about who would be their new leader and were determined to resist his authority. The small congregation had voted four to one against accepting any pastor the Bishop S. M. Crouch might recommend for them.

As Bishop Crouch walked to the podium to introduce young Charles Edward Blake as their new shepherd to the tiny gathering, seven men stood in protest and refused to sit down even after the bishop started talking. Awkward glances flew from face to face. Tense whispers and nervous coughs created a biting buzz throughout the room. As Bishop Crouch raised his hands to hush the antagonistic crowd, young Pastor Blake was quietly questioning his choice of calling.

"Let's all stand together," commanded the elder leader. Surprisingly, everyone obeyed. Then Bishop Crouch slowly approached Pastor Blake, tapped him on the shoulder, pointed to the congregation standing before them and whispered, "It's yours, my boy." Without a glance back over his shoulder, the bishop kept right on walking, down the aisle past the angry members and straight out the sanctuary door. He never came back.

But Pastor Blake stayed put, astutely frozen in his recognition that this must be the church God had been preparing for him since his seminary days at the Interdenominational Theological Center in Southern California. Though the ensuing exchange was difficult and often explosive at his new church, to the point where an armed guard was needed for a time to escort Pastor Blake to his office, young Charles eventually won over the members. They began to see past their personal skepticism to recognize this new pastor was a likable, well-educated and skilled leader whose heart was devoted to God. He was, indeed, at the right place.

"A Church on the Move for God"

Today, Charles Edward Blake has moved up but he has not moved out of the community where his ministry began. He has moved into a higher position now, where he serves as regional bishop for his 90-year-old, 4-million member denomination, overseeing some 250 churches in his West Coast jurisdiction.

Bishop Blake has been recognized as one of America's greatest contemporary black preachers. He is a frequent speaker at Christian conventions and evangelical churches around the world and has been a key figure in the current movement to restore racial reconciliation within and between Pentecostal denominations.

Bishop Blake's own church, West Angeles Church of God in Christ, still located strategically in the heart of South Central Los Angeles, has come a long way since those early, tense days. Now, the church has more than 12,000 active members (including celebrities such as Denzel Washington, Stevie Wonder, Gladys Knight and Magic Johnson) and more than 50 holistic ministries to meet the felt needs of the community. Bishop Blake's leadership has helped make this church the largest and fastest-growing black church in the world.

Bishop Blake's original staff of two has grown to one hundred full-time workers and ministers. More than 1,000 members have joined the church each year just since 1991, and 5 standing-room-only worship services featuring award-winning choirs are offered each Sunday with dozens of other activities provided for members every day of the week.

The small marquee at the church entry on Crenshaw Boulevard reads that this is "A Church on the Move for God." The church is having a big influence in the community and has earned a solid reputation for demonstrating God's love in visible, creative ways. So much so that during the 1992 riots in Los Angeles, while neighboring businesses were either looted or vandalized, no part of West Angeles Church of God in Christ was touched—a credit to the credibility, vision and leadership of the bishop, his staff and its members.

Leaders Need High Standards

As I see it, the qualities of a leader such as Bishop Blake are essential for those of us concerned about leading the Body of Christ at large into positive, effective ministries for the city. At a time when many executive leaders in the world (and sometimes in the church) are without principles and morals, causing widespread injustice and suffering, it is important to find godly leaders who are willing to give the problems and the issues of the inner city priority attention on their busy agendas.

A glance through any daily newspaper will reveal a lack of biblical leadership, evident in many political scandals, incidences of police brutality and corporate failures. These very problems testify to the immoral greed, cruelty and selfishness so often prevalent in our leaders and officials.

My friend Bishop Blake, however, is a refreshing example of what Christian leaders can do when they have spiritual vision, personal integrity and moral excellence. In his almost 30 years of full-time ministry, the bishop has maintained a high standard for both himself and his church, focusing very early on in using the resources of his congregation to meet the felt needs of the contemporary urban dwellers who surround it.

Bishop Blake has nurtured friendships and partnerships with pastors such as Jack Hayford at The Church On The Way, and often finds himself preaching at Korean, white and Hispanic churches throughout the city. In the process, he never imagined his church would grow to such an astonishing number. But, as he puts it, it has happened because "I first looked at the things I wanted to do for the community and realized we'd need a big church to finance those things. I wasn't thinking in terms of a big church, but I did start making every provision for that. We've been blessed to grow and prosper as a church, but growth for growth's sake is not a worthy goal."

Not a Typical Megachurch

As a result of Bishop Blake's early conviction, West Angeles Church of God in Christ is not a "typical" megachurch. The growth that has occurred has not been because it wanted to boast about becoming the world's largest black church. Nor has it grown because of the influence of the church-growth movement to which so many evangelical churches have fallen prey. It has grown because Bishop Blake preached solid, biblical messages and because the congregation made a commitment to meeting the whole needs of its community for the sake of the gospel. The bishop and his staff believe that "a small weak church cannot do great things."

Consequently, the church has tried to maximize the use of personal, organizational and financial resources for the church members and their neighbors. They believe churches must create a sense of community that springs forth from those resources and then sends out members to redeem society. These brothers and sisters are committed to doing everything possible for transforming the life of each person who walks through the door, or in this case, who waits in a line outside that literally wraps around the church building just for the opportunity to enter the sanctuary.

I believe the size of West Angeles Church simply means it has greater potential to influence its community. The exciting challenge for the leaders is tapping into the gifts, talents and resources of those 13,000 members so they can be channeled into Christian community development. That, of course, involves every aspect of life—spiritual, educational, political, social and economic. Dr. Kenneth Hammonds, director of education and training for the church, best exemplified such a tone when he said, "It's an honor to be a part of one of the greatest churches in the world. But it's more wonderful to be saved."

Community Involvement Crucial

It is important for me to note, too, that such a commitment to holistic ministry often brings the blessings of growth in numbers and resources. David Hall of the Church of God in Christ publishing board links blackchurch vitality directly to community involvement with the poor—an obvious hallmark of West Angeles Church.

Every growing church in the denomination, says Hall, has developed some form of community relief efforts. Such emphasis on community service also has been recognized in a study on the black church by the Lilly Endowment Foundation in Indianapolis, Indiana. It found that burgeoning black congregations offer a wide spectrum of services, including job training, counseling and housing-development projects.

The Heart of the City Is the Heart of Ministry

In addition to fully equipping the saints for the ministry, West Angeles Church of God in Christ does not have a shortage of any of these community ministries. Since the bishop and his wife, Mae, came on board in 1969, the church has initiated several services that meet the whole needs of the people in South Central Los Angeles. Though the congregation is comprised of community residents and commuters (some coming from as far away as San Bernardino, Riverside and Ventura counties), the heart of the city is the heart of its ministry.

In some ways, I see West Angeles Church becoming a sort of Renaissance Center, complete with performing arts ministries, musicals, Christian education, food services, Bible classes, economic development, personal counseling and spiritual formation—a center that provides new hope in the midst of an often hopeless neighborhood.

When the Los Angeles riots and protests broke out around the church, the Renaissance Center of West Angeles Church expanded its mission and went to work overtime. It kept its doors open for ongoing prayer services during and after the chaos. Members visited community residents door-to-door, offering prayer and assistance. The youth department organized the involvement of hundreds of youth from throughout the city to help in cleanup efforts, street evangelism, food and clothing distribution and alternative activities. Special counseling services and crisis-management information were offered along with 24-hour prayer lines, unlimited transportation and errand services for the elderly, and funds for those whose businesses were lost in the fires.

The church fed more than 7,000 people through extensive outreach services targeted to Riot Relief—this was in addition to the regular food-services program that provides an average of 5,000 meals monthly through the Skid Row Ministry. Three thousand nine hundred families were assisted with clothing, furniture and relocation needs while church volunteers worked from 5:00 A.M. to 8:00 P.M. daily during the period of civil unrest in the Los Angeles vicinity. The church responded to the neighboring crisis by bringing new hope and a sense of rebirth, or renaissance, for those who were caught in the cross fire of the violent protests.

It is no wonder, then, that church membership has continued to grow at West Angeles Church—there is a place for everyone here to receive ministry and to become ministers. Consequently, the congregation has already outgrown its present $6-million facility. They have plans to build an 8,000-seat complex in the next few years just down the street to better accommodate the growing congregation. A new building, though, won't change the focus or commitments of the people at West Angeles Church of God in Christ. A tour through the present campus on the corner of Crenshaw and Jefferson Boulevards reflects the many functions of this community-minded church.

A Place of Beauty and Function

Across the street from Burger King, Union Bank and a gas station, sits the sanctuary with its adjoining prayer and ministry rooms. This building used to be a furniture store (I bought my family's sofa there when

BEAUTY IS AN ESSENTIAL ATTRIBUTE FOR

THOSE LIVING AND WORKING IN A CITY TOO

OFTEN MADE UGLY BY TRASH, CEMENT AND

SECONDHAND GOODS.

we first moved to California!) and now is a warm, reverent worship center with colorful stained-glass windows. Behind the pews and choir loft are a series of gracefully decorated offices for the ministry staff. Each was designed by the bishop's wife, Mae, and reflects the belief she shares with her husband: Beauty is an essential attribute for those living and working in a city too often made ugly by trash, cement and secondhand goods.

So Mrs. Blake has carefully coordinated each office and hallway to instill a sense of the beautiful. On many walls hang stirring, original paintings done by the bishop's personal aide, Frank Robinson. Whether it is a portrait of Abraham Lincoln or a contemporary version of the Resurrection, Brother Robinson's paintings provide additional complements to Mrs. Blake's designs, both communicating a message of dignity and respect to all who enter.

Next door is the Crystal Room, a huge, elegant multipurpose room complete with full-service kitchen facilities (but no plastic cutlery) and a few television monitors. The Crystal Room is used for anything from overflow worship services to wedding receptions to local business luncheons.

On the second floor above the Crystal Room are more offices, classrooms for the Bible college and Christian-education department, and meeting rooms for special workshops and fellowship.

Around the corner, in what was once a bar, is the church bookstore, the distribution office for the food and Skid Row Ministry and an inviting counseling center (which used to be a Japanese restaurant). Here, professional and trained lay counselors serve an average of 1,500 people each year free of charge in individual and family sessions, as well as in a variety of support groups ranging from AIDS awareness and codependency to single parenting and suicide prevention. The counseling center, directed by Dr. Mardra Paredes, also offers a 24-hour prayer line that has lay counselors available, and conferences and seminars throughout the year.

West Angeles Christian Academy

Directly across Crenshaw Boulevard from the counseling center, more than 250 children dressed in red-and-blue uniforms fill the classrooms and halls of the K-8 elementary school known as West Angeles Christian Academy. Founded in 1976 by Bishop and Mrs. Blake to fulfill the axiom of "teaching children daily in the temple," the Academy, like the church, has seen a steady increase in enrollment ever since.

Hope Gordon, the principal of the Academy, says children come here from throughout Los Angeles because their parents understand that the Academy is "providing training in the Word of God, stressing academic excellence, personal achievement, developing personal discipline and respect for authority." To reinforce this, on the wall in the eighth-grade classroom hangs a sign that says "Discipline, Dedication, Determination equals Excellence." And these eighth-graders are taking that challenge seriously. They have raised enough money for a class trip to Paris where they will study culture, art, history and government.

In addition to international travel and general course work, students participate in an African-American cultural awareness program, journalism classes, outdoor science-education programs at Angeles Crest National Forest, after-school sports programs, recreational and cultural field trips and, of course, daily Bible study.

Says one seventh-grade student, "I feel like I'm very lucky to be at a Christian school. People look at us like we're small, but, you know, it's a very good school." The school's dedication has paid off because most WACA students go on to graduate from high school and attend college. And one former student is currently attending Harvard.

Christian Arts Center

A few yards from the Academy is the Christian Arts Center. The 500-seat auditorium, which used to be a Japanese cultural center, now offers concerts, plays, Christian comedy nights and original musicals throughout the year.

Hollywood actor-producer-director and West Angeles church member, Robert Townsend (the "Meteor Man") has already produced a number of Christian shows here with the hopes that the Arts Center will become a quality, competitive theater known throughout the city. The Arts Center also hosts a weekly Spanish-speaking congregation to meet the changing ethnic character of the Crenshaw corridor.

An Effective, Competent Staff

But it is the people, not the facilities, at West Angeles Church of God in Christ who really bring new life to their community. Almost all of Bishop Blake's interracial staff hold bachelor's degrees, many have master's degrees and several live within walking distance of the church. They are gracious, articulate and take seriously the vision and ministry their pastor has instilled in them. Together, they form a competent, effective team that has helped its congregation influence its city for Christ in powerful ways.

I am personally encouraged by the team of workers at West Angeles and see its continuing commitment to holistic ministries and Christian community development as positive examples of what megachurches can do.

Community Action Teams

My friend Lula Bailey Ballton is executive director of West Angeles Community Development Corporation. She and I have worked together for the last few years to help the church establish a more firm foundation for its social-service ministries. Not only have I had the privilege of preaching at West Angeles Church worship services, I have also been able to lead Christian Community Development workshops

"GOD HAS CALLED WEST ANGELES COMMUNITY DEVELOPMENT CORPORATION TO PROMOTE JUSTICE AND PEACE, DEMONSTRATE COMPASSION AND ERADICATE POVERTY AS TANGIBLE EXPRESSIONS OF THE KINGDOM OF GOD THROUGH THE VEHICLE OF COMMUNITY DEVELOPMENT."

for the people involved in such outreach. Consequently, I have watched Lula and her team grow in their vision and influence for their surrounding neighborhood.

The mission statement reads, "God has called West Angeles Community Development Corporation to promote justice and peace, demonstrate compassion and eradicate poverty as tangible expressions of the Kingdom of God through the vehicle of community development." Lula and her staff of five full-time workers and hundreds of volunteers who comprise Community Action Teams (CATs) have committed themselves to economic empowerment, social justice and community transformation.

The Community Development Corporation (CDC) has initiated programs that include job training, entrepreneurial development, property management, housing development, community dispute resolution, legal services, an adult learning center that includes English as a Second Language, computer training and individual tutoring, and technical assistance for several other churches and organizations committed to Christian community development.

CDC is also partnering with major corporations and businesses to provide employment for underemployed residents and youth. And West Angeles Literacy Empowerment Team (WALET) works directly with local libraries to provide trained, certified tutors for youth or adults needing to improve their reading and writing skills. Their mission? "To glorify God through Christian activities and behaviors dedicated to rid illiteracy in South Central Los Angeles."

But working for change in the community has always been a concern for Lula, so she was a natural fit for this position. Lula has a J.D. degree from UCLA School of Law and a master's in communication from Northwestern University in Chicago, so she is well qualified to lead the CDC. But she has had a personal passion for justice and peace since the 1960s.

Lula came to Los Angeles in 1965 to attend college. The day she arrived was the day the race riots occurred. She left four years later when she graduated and didn't return until 1980. Ever since then, she and her husband and three children have been members of West Angeles Church. She worked for a corporate law firm before accepting the Lord's call to the Union Rescue Mission.

When Bishop Blake felt the need to incorporate all the social services at West Angeles under an umbrella organization such as the CDC, he knew exactly who could run it. He knew Lula had been becoming more and more committed to seeing Christian community-development ministry organized from the church. So Lula left her law firm and work at the Mission to help found and oversee the CDC.

"Even though I was 40 when I went to law school, I always knew I was going to be an advocate for the poor," says Lula. "Now, though, I have a biblical perspective for that. Of course, the main work of the church is to serve members but CDC helps these people utilize their skills. I think we're on the cutting edge in light of serving the poor and providing a new alternative to welfare."

Because all of Lula's staff lives in the neighborhood, she believes it is easier for them to identify with and assess the felt needs. "We all came home to bring the resources and the CDC to the community. We don't need to learn a new language; we *are* the language and the community."

Personalized Ministry

This focus on social justice and spiritual growth is a natural extension of the church's mission to evangelize the city. And that has been particularly good news for one young woman named Deborah. Deborah was not a Christian when she first called the CDC office to see if anyone might be interested in helping her take meals to homebound AIDS patients in Hollywood. She told Claudia, Lula's assistant, about Project Angel Food (PAF) and about how hard it was to get people from the area to help deliver meals.

Claudia then invited Deborah to present her appeal at one of the Community Action Team meetings and to meet Lula. She got involved in the CDC ministry, the church helped her with PAF, and all along, Claudia kept inviting her to church. After watching these Christians in action, Deborah finally attended a worship service where, as Lula put it, "Something happened for her and she prayed the Sinner's Prayer."

A young man named Bobby was a student in the summer employment program. Often, he would complain to Lula that the workers were "bugging me about Jesus." Lula encouraged him to hang in there; he did, after all, have a good job. Then the summer ended and he went back to school.

Months later, Lula was surprised to see Bobby show up to volunteer. He came the next week and the next week. "Now we can't get rid of the kid," Lula laughs. "You see, this is our community. We don't soft-pedal the people here; we just love them. That's why people like Bobby come back."

The Whole Gospel for the Whole Community

And all these activities and the neighborhood involvement are exactly what Bishop Blake has hoped would happen all along. Though he, his staff and the church's members know there are always going to be battles, they are committed to bringing the whole gospel to their whole community. Because of that, I believe West Angeles Church of God in Christ is a wonderful example of redistribution and Christian community development.

Their example has evolved because, as the Bishop says, "We've tried always to honor the biblical fundamentals, to retain the core values of God's Word while attempting to have a sensitivity to the needs and aspirations to this day, all the while maintaining a contemporary witness that hopefully is making a difference in the lives of many people. We want to make a social, structural, spiritual and organizational impact on our community." From the looks of things, that is exactly what is happening.

Taking It to the Streets

In the midst of riot-torn South Central Los Angeles, West Angeles Church of God in Christ is committed to the Christian community development principle of redistribution. Bishop Blake has always wanted to meet the felt needs of his urban community and so has prayed that God would bring the resources and the personnel to his church to do just that. God, no doubt, has answered.

It is almost overwhelming to see all this church is doing. Without question, its influence in education, food distribution, counseling, worship and economic development, discipleship and evangelism can be felt throughout the city. But the grace and dignity that the staff and members of West Angeles exude is just as noticeable, giving this congregation a witness and a testimony that is both credible and empowering. This is a people who give of themselves in the midst of a city that has many, many needs. That's why I firmly believe their gifts will have eternal rewards and many earthly benefits.

How can you be a part of the process of redistribution? What talents, gifts and resources can you help channel to best meet the needs of your local urban community?

I pray that God will direct you and your church to give gifts that will change present conditions while reaping eternal blessings.

Manhattan Transformation

*Proverbs 11:10 says, "When the righteous prosper,
the city rejoices." Pastor Tim Keller and his congregation
at Redeemer Presbyterian Church in Manhattan, New
York, have taken this verse to heart and asked God and
themselves what their church needs to be to make all of
New York City rejoice. Consequently, they have become
a unique and powerful model for redistribution
and Christian community development.*

New York City's Diversity

If you have ever been to New York City, you know it is unlike any
other place in the world. Some people say New York City *is* the
world crammed into blocks and blocks of high-rises, hotels and har-
ried hangouts.

Every time I visit and walk down Broadway or Eighth Avenue (or
anywhere else in Manhattan for that matter), and sit on the subway or
in a Yellow cab, I am bombarded with the depth of God's creativity literally staring me in the face: Ethiopians, Jamaicans, yuppies, Chinese,
Latinos, punk rockers, Africans, Southern belles, homeless, Russian
Jews, elderly, Irish and Japanese. The list goes on as the whole world
walks past. From this incredible array of diversity, I realize this is a
city that seems to have no majority culture, class or religion.

To be sure, America has become a nation of nations and I doubt any
city better exemplifies this truth than Manhattan. Really, the wonderful cultural diversity that fills this urban sprawl known as the "Big
Apple" defines the very mission of our country's existence. Lady
Liberty has welcomed the tired and poor, the huddled masses yearning
to come from distant shores and enjoy the opportunities our free coun-

try affords them. We are a nation of diverse cultures and New York is a microcosm of that. Both are a result of our creative God.

Unfortunately, though, we have also become a nation of strangers. Economic, technological and cultural attitudes have pushed us farther and farther from one another, creating discrepancies and injustices that often ignore the biblical mandate to care for one another out of the resources God has given us. Let's face it: In spite of all the wonderful things about our country, we also are a nation of convenience where it's much easier to stay in the confines of our predictable lifestyles than to cross cultural lines by reaching out to the various people groups God has brought to the United States.

Unless, of course, you live in New York City. You merely have to walk outside your home here to cross economic and cultural lines. In Manhattan, every day you see the reality that nations and resources walk side by side with nomads and the poor. New Yorkers come face-to-face daily with people in need—the homeless street hawker, the struggling single parent, the bewildered new immigrant or the hollow-eyed victim of AIDS. This is a city where the extraordinary appears ordinary, a city that never sleeps, a city full of problems and programs, pain and plenty—and one, thankfully, that God's people have not abandoned.

Redeemer's "Yuppies"

Drawing on the natural human resources of this international city is a unique, six-year-old congregation known as Redeemer Presbyterian Church (PCA). It is both a center-city church and a church without walls. Meetings are held two times on Sundays in the auditorium of Hunter College at East 69th between Park and Lexington Avenues for a liturgical and a contemporary jazz service, and throughout the week at homes, offices and restaurants around Manhattan.

Redeemer Presbyterian is not a commuter church because 80 percent of the 1,500 multicultural members live within close walking or subway distance. And its primary target group is one often ignored by evangelical churches in New York City—young single urban professionals. Each week, they come faithfully from all walks of New York life: editors, teachers, actors, engineers, fashion designers, Wall Street brokers, musicians, accountants, graduate students, activists, artists and attorneys. And these New York "yuppies" come to Redeemer full of life, skills, zeal and questions. Lots of questions.

Redeemer's Birth

Forty-four-year-old Senior Pastor Tim Keller expected this "questioning" scenario when he helped found Redeemer Presbyterian in the fall of 1989. He had done his demographic homework and was well aware what a ministry would have to look like to reach the educated, talented professionals who lived in Manhattan—a segment of the population other churches and ministries had often overlooked.

It started when Keller, his wife, Kathy, and their three sons were living in Philadelphia. Friends in Manhattan called them, asking them to consider planting a church here. Pastor Keller was content in teaching leadership and preaching classes at Westminster Theological Seminary and so he wished his friends well in their attempt to find a pastor. He did offer, though, to help by doing field research for them and for a colleague who was planting a Chinese church in New York City.

As Keller studied the demographics of the Big Apple, he was admittedly "awed and stirred by the arrogance, fierce secularity, diversity, power and spiritual barrenness of New York City." He quickly realized that a center-city church of professionals could provide muchneeded resources and opportunities to meet the diverse felt needs of Manhattan residents.

By June 1988, after several unsuccessful attempts to recruit other church planters, the Kellers committed to moving their family to New York City to plant a Presbyterian church. They gathered a core group of committed Christians and began networking the city, looking specifically for new Christians for two reasons: They had little church affiliation and they were most likely still in relationships with non-Christians.

Early on in their field research, the Kellers met with workers from local parachurch ministries who were seeing conversions among Manhattan's professionals and started networking with them as well. They requested and received prayer and financial support from their denomination, knowing prayer from dozens of other churches throughout the country would lay a firm foundation for them.

The core group then started meeting together in one couple's Manhattan apartment for its own time of prayer and vision setting. From those meetings, these people developed an outline for building a church that would reach New York's urban professionals. They concluded that the services had to be warm but dignified and had to continue with historic liturgical forms because most of the folks they were trying to reach loved the theatre, art galleries and symphony halls. They also recognized that the preaching had to be intelligent, bordering on the intellectual but showing familiarity with urban-life issues. Says Pastor Keller, "We decided always to present the classic Christian message in close connection with the issues we identified as 'burning and relevant' to the average Manhattanite."

The team also recognized that all outreach should only be through friendship networking so they decided not to do any advertising. Instead, they simply encouraged friends to invite friends, keeping relationship-building and lay leadership as the heart of the church.

They started small-group fellowships for personal care and mutual

▐█

REDEEMER PRESBYTERIAN CHURCH

WAS BORN WITH ONE CLEAR PURPOSE:

"TO BRING THE RESOURCES OF THE HISTORIC

CHRISTIAN FAITH TO BEAR ON NEW YORK CITY

UNTIL WE ARE MAKING A VISIBLE DIFFERENCE IN

THE QUALITY OF ITS LIFE—SPIRITUALLY,

SOCIALLY, MATERIALLY."

▐█

support. Redeemer leaders knew early on that once these professionals came to hear the gospel at either a worship service or a home group, they could emphasize their purpose for ministry within the city.

The church quickly became recognized as an equipping center for people who wanted to meet a variety of needs throughout New York. Consequently, the Kellers and their friends understood that if they could continue building caring relationships, preaching the gospel with relevance and intelligence, and stressing ministry and volunteerism, they would tap into incredible opportunities to transform Manhattan for Jesus Christ.

Training Servant-Leaders

So from a small prayer group in an Eastside apartment that met in the spring of 1989, along with a handful of committed folks, Redeemer Presbyterian Church was born with one clear purpose: "To bring the resources of the historic Christian faith to bear on New York City until we are making a visible difference in the quality of its life—spiritually, socially, materially." They started with 60 people at the first service and grew to 300 within several months. Now, Redeemer has more than 1,500 people from all careers and cultures coming to its services.

Although the group owns no building and probably never will, and because Redeemer does not exist simply to satisfy the needs of its members, I believe it is an excellent example of a contemporary church committed to the values of redistribution and Christian community development. I know that Pastor Keller and his staff of 12 hope their urban neighbors will perceive Redeemer as a resource church as well as an incubator for training servant-leaders to go into the city and demonstrate the gospel to fellow New Yorkers. In short, they hope Redeemer helps establish "a vital link between God and the human heart...between Christians and the city."

Vital Links

Forty-year-old Tony Santiago experienced firsthand that "vital link." He grew up in the city and had had enough of the busyness, the crowds and the noise. He wanted out. Then, one Sunday morning, he heard Pastor Keller's sermon on why they were placed so strategically in Manhattan, and Tony's heart was changed. "I was ready to leave [the city] when I first visited Redeemer. Now I see that I need to be here to help change the city, to help connect people to Christ."

Joe and Connie Ricci have a similar story. They had both come to New York to pursue acting careers, intent on making it big and then leaving the city. Though they became Christians in New York, they were still convinced that retreating to a more comfortable place far away beat city life—until they heard Pastor Keller preach on God's heart for the city.

"That sermon made us realize we had been selfish and we needed to stay here long term," the couple wrote in a letter to the pastor. "Your 'city' sermon was the spanking we needed to turn our heads in a circle. Now with Junior on the way we are here indefinitely to follow God's will and not our own. And my sister has become a Christian and is coming to NYC as well."

The City Rejoices

It is precisely this kind of influence that has made Proverbs 11:10 such a significant verse for my friends in New York City: "When the right-eous prosper, the city rejoices."

Ever since the church started, Redeemer leaders have viewed Proverbs 11:10 as instrumental in determining how they could best influ-ence their city for Christ. Pastor Keller remembers how this verse caused him to ask, "What kind of church would we have to be so that virtually the entire city of New York would rejoice that we are in its midst?" As a result, they knew they wanted to be a church that made New York City literally rejoice at their presence. Pastor Keller's question, they say, is what shapes their congregation today, as well as their decisions and strategies for reaching the city through a variety of exciting ministries.

The Nerve System of Redeemer

One essential ministry at Redeemer Presbyterian was created early on because these folks recognized the need to nurture personal, meaning-ful relationships. They understood that because New York City is so densely populated and so transient, it is often difficult to maintain sig-nificant friendships. Redeemer's solution was to build an intense net-work of home-group fellowships while simultaneously training small-group leaders. These communities of 6 to 12 people encourage partic-ipants to grow in their knowledge of, and relationship with, God.

The groups also inspire growth in character and service through prayer and mutual encouragement. This happens so much that "while some congregations have some small-group meetings or Bible studies," reads their visitor's brochure, "our congregation *is* a collection of small groups. Home groups serve as the 'nerve' system of our church...the primary place for care."

As Jeff White, the associate pastor, says, "We have a very strong intention to make the gospel accessible to people who haven't entered church doors in years. We remember what it was like not to believe so we want to treat people with respect in our homes and services."

Spiritual Wholeness Through Counseling

White's attitude also translates into many support groups through the supervision of Redeemer's counseling staff. Early members will tell you that choosing Redeemer as the name of their church was perfect for a city whose residents knew they needed transformation.

"People in the city often have an awful past," says one staff member. "Redeemer means hope for those regardless of what they have done. We have had people coming here out of all sorts of situations, mate swapping, pornographic filmmaking, drug abuse, you name it."

To best offer change and redemption to its diverse congregation, Redeemer has organized many support groups, ranging in issues from divorce recovery to HIV to eating disorders to 12-step groups. These confidential gatherings provide other meaningful ways for New Yorkers to receive spiritual wholeness while developing their fullest potential in their relationships with God.

From Stardom to Christianity

One young woman in particular is eternally grateful for the home-fellowship group to which she belongs. Lynette came to New York from Dallas, Texas, like so many others, full of dreams and vision and ambition. She was planning to make it big as an actress. It was what she had always wanted to do, and she studied hard in college so she could pursue her dream.

When Lynette came to Manhattan, she found an apartment, a part-time job as a waitress to pay the bills, and then set out to audition her way to stardom. After two years and only a few small parts off Broadway, Lynette was discouraged. She felt empty, shallow and silly for coming to New York. Now she was directionless as well.

Then some Redeemer members visited the restaurant where Lynette worked. They treated her with dignity, told her the truth of Jesus Christ's love for her and invited her to their home-fellowship group. They also left a big tip for her. To their surprise, Lynette came to their small group, full of questions.

After weeks of honest dialogue and serious Bible study, the group encouraged Lynette to attend Redeemer's class called "Discovering Christianity." In the seven-week course, the class addressed questions such as, Why believe in God? Why believe in the Bible? Will it be good for me to believe? How do I become a Christian? All along, Lynette never stopped attending the small-group home fellowship. As a result of both groups, Lynette entered into a personal commitment to Jesus Christ, thankful that her new family of friends had loved her into God's kingdom. She then moved into Redeemer's Sunday-morning Foundations class, where she studied a how-to course on living the Christian life.

Lynette's story is not unlike so many others who have come to eternal decisions through the small-group ministry of Redeemer Presbyterian. Here they find answers to painful, plaguing questions. Pastor Keller intentionally scheduled Sunday School classes to be held after the worship services so he and his staff could address questions visitors might have about his sermons.

"We hope not just to produce converts, but to produce a praising people," says Pastor Keller. "We believe whatever it is you worship is the definition of your own personality. So the only way to change someone is to change what they worship."

Janet Grams is grateful for the solid biblical teaching she receives at Redeemer Presbyterian because she knows how much it has changed

■

"WE WANT TO BE ABOUT DEVELOPING CULTURAL LEADERS WHO NOT ONLY CARE ABOUT THE POOR, BUT ALSO LEARN FROM THEM AND PARTNER WITH THEM AS BROTHERS AND SISTERS IN CHRIST. I DON'T KNOW HOW YOU CAN BRIDGE THE GAP BETWEEN THE POOR AND ELITE UNLESS YOU HAVE THE GOSPEL."

■

her. "When I started coming here, I had just left a sad relationship," she recalls. "Coming here, though, I get fed. It's helped me get my eyes off myself and has shown me how to give. Learning from these pastors has really helped."

As a full-time staff worker with Campus Crusade's Here's Life Inner City, Janet knows how demanding and how difficult life can be in New York. For her, Redeemer is a place of worship that is both refreshing and challenging.

Redeemer Cares for Neighbors' Holistic Needs

Everyone who attends Redeemer also knows it is a place that is passionate about caring for the holistic needs of its neighbors. To Pastor Keller, the top 20 percent of leaders from the "secular cultural elite" don't always care about the poor or the underclass. He also believes most don't want to learn from the poor because they are "too religious.

To the cultural elite, the poor say 'Hallelujah' because they don't know any better," says the senior pastor. "But we want to be about developing cultural leaders who not only care about the poor, but also learn from them and partner with them as brothers and sisters in Christ. I don't know how you can bridge the gap between the poor and elite unless you have the gospel."

Because of Pastor Keller's goal for Redeemer, the church sent a dozen members to our sixth-annual Christian Community Development Association (CCDA) conference in Baltimore in 1994. Because the Big Apple doesn't provide many CCDA members, the church wanted to learn firsthand what it meant for it to be committed to holistic ministry throughout the city. Although I know this church has long been involved in social ministry around the city and the world (it has regularly sent ministry teams to its sister church, New Song Community Church, to work with Sandtown's Habitat for Humanity in Baltimore), its members recognize the need for more education on how to implement CCDA principles.

Redeemer is sending two couples to live and work with CCDA churches so they can return in a few years to develop similar works in Manhattan. John and Melanie Acevedo are heading to Pastor Noel Castellanos's church, La Villita Community Church in Chicago, and Jim and Michelle Pickett are already going through training at New City Fellowship in Chattanooga, Tennessee. In this way, Redeemer can be "the kind of place where we incubate a vision for Christian community development and spawn and partner with new works," says Pastor Keller.

Hope for New York

Longtime Redeemer staff member Yvonne Dodd couldn't agree more. Recently elected to serve on our national CCDA board, Yvonne is president of Hope for New York, the mercy ministry arm of Redeemer Presbyterian. Her primary responsibility is to encourage and channel Redeemer members into many social ministries throughout New York City. But CCDA helped prepare the way for Yvonne.

When Redeemer Church promoted Yvonne to her current position, it also sent her out to research other churches' ministries. She and Pastor Keller had discussed the possibility of having a mercy-ministry arm since the church began. So she started looking at ministry models to determine what would work in Manhattan, as every place differs from the other.

To research ministries committed to the principles of Christian community development, Yvonne visited Lawndale Community Church
and La Villita Community Church, the Mid-America Leadership
Foundation and Circle Urban Ministries, all in Chicago, New Song
Community Church in Baltimore, Jubilee Ministries in Washington,
D.C., and FCS Urban Ministries in Atlanta. Instead of duplicating
these efforts, though, Yvonne believed coming alongside already existing ministries would be more beneficial in New York. As a result, they
set up Hope for New York.

"New York City as a culture is predisposed to the idea of volunteerism because of the liberal bent to help in the city," Yvonne says.
"Hope for New York is just part of the incubator. It gets people
involved in the needs of the city and gets them started while bringing
them out of their shell."

Although it has not always been easy, Yvonne is trying to capitalize
on the strengths of the people at Redeemer, to get people "to stick their
toes into the water. A lot of members are brand-new Christians or
'recovering' Christians who came to New York City to escape. But
God's providence and their circumstances brought them back."

In just two years, Yvonne has seen Hope for New York grow into a
powerful force of 225 volunteers serving in 12 mercy ministries
throughout the city. She sees her role as one where she is "to light
fires" under members, to get them involved in existing ministries and
to be partners with them. The resources at Redeemer are great, she
says, because Redeemer has a lot of folks who have MBAs, as well as
electricians, administrators, lawyers, accountants, fund-raisers, writers
and photographers.

"Just the kind of people who can help run ministries from a business technical perspective," says Yvonne. "So we really do partner. We
don't just give money, we give expertise and volunteers to partner with
these other believers who are in the trenches. And everyone benefits."

These volunteers have plenty of opportunities to transform New
York by demonstrating God's love. They lead Bible studies at the
Bowery Mission Men's Transitional Center, serve meals to people with
AIDS through the Friends Ministry, teach English to Russian Jews
through the Russian Literacy Project, and provide training for job
skills through Sonshines Services and the Hope Christian Center.
They serve coffee and exchange conversation with homeless friends at
St. Paul's House and The Lamb's, counsel pregnant women at the
Midtown Pregnancy Support Center and Bowery Women's Center,
and tutor inner-city children through Operation Exodus Inner City

and East Harlem Little League. I believe these unique partnerships Redeemer has established with such Christian ministries has given New York City many more reasons to rejoice at its presence.

Volunteering That Changes You

Hope for New York has also given its members, as well as its neighbors in need, reason to rejoice. Jay Easterling is a white former football player from Mississippi who came to Manhattan to work for IBM. Yvonne met him at Redeemer and she quickly invited him to serve on the board of Hope for New York. Although Jay grew up in the South, he hadn't thought much about racial issues or social injustices. He didn't have to. But now that he is on the board, he says his life is different.

Once a week, Jay goes to the Bowery Mission to facilitate a mentoring Bible study with the homeless men there. They talk about what it means to be a Christian man, and study Scriptures that help shape their identities in Christ. Because of the effective ministry record of the Bowery Mission, this is one of the few Christian discipleship programs that is fully funded by the city government. As a result of volunteering there, Jay has discovered, "There's no difference between men who are homeless, ex-cons and MBAs. I look at the world with different eyes now." Now he's recruiting others to get involved, to become Christian witnesses who care deeply about their city.

A Big Heart in the Big Apple

There is no doubt in my mind that Redeemer Presbyterian Church in Manhattan is a unique and powerful example of what can happen when God's people see their resources as opportunities to redeem their city. Here is a congregation with no building, yet it is still going out to serve its community. It is a church that hopes to plant hundreds and hundreds of similar churches throughout the international community of New York. It is a congregation of Christians who know who they are and how God wants to lead them as together they transform Manhattan.

As Pastor Keller puts it, "We're humbly seeking to be servants and catalysts for Christian community development. We haven't done enough yet but we're on a pilgrimage, and open to change. Really, we'd like to be a big heart, an engine that sucks people in and then sends them right back out."

Taking It to the Streets

Redeemer Presbyterian uniquely utilizes its diverse resources to help reach New York City for Christ. Pastor Keller and his staff have a clear sense of purpose, identity and mission for their church: to show urban professionals God's love and then channel their talents into positive directions to change the city for Christ.

I think one of the greatest things about Redeemer is its commitment to developing friendships. Its small groups are the backbone of this contemporary church, providing both great personal care and incredible collaborative opportunities for service and community development. I believe this is what being a part of God's family is all about.

How could you help network people in your city to hear the gospel and to respond to its life-changing message? What could your church be doing so that the community where you live "rejoices" at your presence?

I pray that God will lead you to develop strong, mutual Christian friendships as together you witness to your city of the transforming power of God's love.

CONCLUSION

There *Is* a Balm

*My sorrow is beyond healing, My heart is faint within
me! Behold, listen! The cry of the daughter of my people from
a distant land: "Is the Lord not in Zion? Is her King not within her? Why have they provoked Me with their graven images,
with foreign idols? Harvest is past, summer is ended, and we
are not saved." For the brokenness of the daughter of my people I am broken; I mourn, dismay has taken hold of me.*
**Is there no balm in Gilead?
Is there no physician there?** *Why then has not the health
of the daughter of my people been restored? Oh, that my
head were waters, and my eyes a fountain of tears, that I
might weep day and night for the slain of the daughter of
my people! O that I had in the desert a wayfarers' lodging
place; that I might leave my people, and go from them! For
all of them are adulterers, an assembly of treacherous men.
"And they bend their tongue like their bow; lies and not
truth prevail in the land; for they proceed from evil to evil,
and they do not know Me," declares the Lord.*

Thus cried the prophet Jeremiah in chapters 8:18—9:3 (*NASB*,
emphasis added). Jeremiah's grief was for his people who were caught
in the calamity and ruin of their city; his despair was for the horrible
conditions that had taken hold of their land.

It seemed that Jeremiah refused to be comforted as he cried out to
God to bring healing and restoration to the people who were trapped
in lies, evil and injustice, and who did not know God. He looked upon
the situation as deplorable, almost beyond relief, wondering if perhaps
the desolations of Gilead were irreparable. Perhaps Jeremiah was lay-

ing blame for the seemingly incurable social diseases on the people themselves, implying that the only balm in Gilead, the only physician able to bring healing, was God Himself.

THE MISERIES OF OUR COUNTRY OUGHT TO BECOME THE GRIEF OF OUR SOULS. THEY OUGHT TO SHOW US THAT CURES ARE AVAILABLE *ONLY IF* GOD'S PEOPLE WILL BEGIN TO ACT AGAIN AS THE CHURCH WAS INTENDED TO ACT IN PROVIDING HOLISTIC SOLUTIONS TO THE PROBLEMS AT HAND.

Yes, certainly Jeremiah understood that God was able to heal His people, and more than sufficient to redress all their grievances. They did, after all, have among them God's laws and prophets to help bring about such change. They did have access to the great physician, and they had a governing force of leaders whose business it was to reform the nation. Why, then, was their health not restored? It was not for want of a balm or a physician. Perhaps it was because they would not admit the application nor submit to the methods of cure. God, the physician, was ready to heal; the people, though, His people, did not understand His ways. And so the great prophet wept about the crisis at hand.

Contemporary Wounds

In many ways, the plight of Jeremiah's people is much like the plight of our own in America's inner cities today. Problems abound in every city, on every street corner. Children are without fathers, young girls are having babies, mothers are strung out on crack and men can't find decent jobs to support their families. We are all concerned with the waste and destruction of the conditions in the urban community, conditions that are dragging down the entire nation. Many people blame the problems on those who live in the inner cities, yet the bureaucratic and impersonal government is also responsible because it rewards the girls who have babies and the men who leave home. We also need to recognize that the Church and the way it has served the poor has often compounded the problems in the cities. Because many Christians have removed themselves from these problems, they have not been available to apply any biblical solutions.

I believe the Church's retreat to suburbia and its obsession with church growth, combined with the government's superficial "solutions," have helped to make the problems of our cities worse. When certain white congregations, along with middle-class blacks, moved away from the urban communities to the suburbs to build comfortable lifestyles and homogeneous congregations, they kept their sense of superiority, disengaging themselves from the issues of the poor and the urban community.

But the problems don't end there. Of course, I believe the sins of the people in the cities are also a factor. If we as Christians see ourselves as the salt of the earth, however, something has to change. Yes, the problem lies in the sinful nature of humans; the lack of the solution lies with the Church because it has too often withdrawn from its mandate to minister.

Like Jeremiah, however, the miseries of our country ought to become the grief of our souls. They ought to show us that cures are available *only if* God's people will begin to act again as the Church was intended to act in providing holistic solutions to the problems at hand. And like Jeremiah, we ought to know that God is ready to apply the healing ointments to our cities in crisis if we are willing to submit to His methods.

I thank God that several congregations of Christians have begun to apply such healing balms to their urban communities across the country. From Redeemer Presbyterian in New York to West Angeles Church of God in Christ in Los Angeles, California, to Lawndale Community Church in Chicago, Illinois, God's people are showing the world that there is a balm in Gilead, there is a physician who will bring restoration.

And God is bringing restoration through simple, human lives, through people who are willing to sacrifice for the sake of the gospel. These people remind us that we as Christians already have the solutions to the urban crisis: Christ is in us as the hope of glory, living out His life through us. Therefore, we can no longer simply pray for God to do something in our cities; we must pray for God to energize *us* to do something. We must be available to His Spirit to do His work in the land.

Our Healing Purpose

We would do well to remember, too, the purpose of a balm in biblical days. Grown in the land of Gilead, balm was a well-known healing oil, used by all kinds of people. Everyone who traveled probably used this oil on trips. In fact, it became interchangeable with the garment in which it was carried, almost like a first-aid kit. It was the provision everyone had in case any ailments or injuries occurred along their travels. Everyone knew that a balm meant healing.

Today, we would define a balm as a small evergreen, an African or Asian tree that has aromatic leaves; an agent that soothes, relieves or

AS WE LOOK AT OUR COUNTRY, WE SEE THE

QUICK REJECTION OF THE LIBERAL DEMOCRATIC

FIX FOR SOCIETY, AND CONSERVATIVES NOT

HAVING MANY NEW SOLUTIONS FOR CHANGE.

THUS, THE CHURCH IS IN A PRIME PLACE TO

INFLUENCE THE COUNTRY.

heals, usually aromatic, soothing and restorative. The purpose of the Christian Church is to be such a balm, one that soothes, relieves or heals; one that gives off the aroma of Christ, and that acts as a restorative agent for people who might feel hurt or injured on their lives' travels. The Church has always been called to be such a balm. Although we have a long way to go in living in such a way today, we must not forget our purpose as God's agents of healing and restoration.

The unique time in which we live is ripe with opportunities for Christians to act as restorative agents. Of course, no one would argue that we live in a time when our country is seeking answers, solutions and change for our cities. Like Jeremiah, many are asking if there is a balm strong enough to heal the ghettos. Sadly, many would say there is no hope, that the cities are beyond repair and that the Church is too removed.

As we look at our country, we see the quick rejection of the liberal democratic fix for society, and conservatives not having many new solutions for change. Thus, the Church is in a prime place to influence the country. I believe this is just the opportunity we need to bring the healing message of the gospel to society, to be the Church again.

And the powerful stories of the congregations in this book prove Christians can make a difference in culturally and economically diverse urban communities. In practical, loving ways, these congregations testify to the mission and love of Jesus Christ.

From Church in the City, Mississippi Boulevard Christian Church, New Song Community Church and Lawndale Community Church, we see the visible demonstration of God's love as His people have relocated to some of America's toughest neighborhoods.

From Mendenhall Bible Church and Voice of Calvary Fellowship, First Baptist Church of Flushing and The Chapel and Arlington Road Church of God partnership, we see the power of God's transcending love in reconciled relationships.

And from Lake Avenue Congregational, West Angeles Church of God in Christ and Redeemer Presbyterian Church, we see biblical justice lived out as these Christians seek creative ways to share resources with their neighbors through the ministry of redistribution.

The stories of these churches are both inspiring and encouraging to those of us who have long cried to God to bring about positive change in our urban neighborhoods.

Jeremiah's Personal Pain

Without question, each story, each testimony from these brothers and sisters has brought great encouragement to me personally. Why? Because I have often felt the same pain for the people that Jeremiah felt. God called him and sent him to be a prophet to his nation even when God's judgment was certain to be on them. Yet, the people had turned against God's goodness, grace and mercy. Still, Jeremiah loved his nation, and was frustrated in seeing its condition.

When Jeremiah asked the questions, "Is there no balm in Gilead? Is there no physician there?" he recognized that something was not working—the balms that had been applied were not the right ones to bring about healing; the physicians at work in the land did not bring about a wholesome change.

I, too, see our cities filled with social organizations and government agencies, plenty of balms and physicians. Yet, I have to ask why my people are still not being healed. Is it because, as Jeremiah recognized, the people proceed from evil to evil, not knowing their God? Is it because the Christian presence as a whole has not applied the ointment of God's healing truth and love to our neighbors in the inner cities? I think these are part of the problems.

But I, like Jeremiah, still have hope. We must conclude that there is a balm. God Himself is working through churches, such as the ones in this book, and hundreds of other willing Christian servants through a movement such as the Christian Community Development Association to restore the land.

These 12 churches have captured the essence of the gospel for our generation and the next. Their leaders are gifted Christian men and women who could be doing almost anything else, but they have chosen to empty their lives for the sake of their people. Consequently, they exude a deep humility and genuine Christlike character, two qualities essential for directing their congregations. Many times, leaders come into a community and exploit the ignorance of the ghetto. But the leaders of these churches are highly intelligent, wanting only to serve out of their humility.

Throughout missionary history, I've noticed that God has always sent out the best—the cream of the crop—to the neediest parts of the world. We need intelligent, articulate people in the ghetto today as well. The leaders of the churches in this book are just that. Their example is inspiring to us all and certainly worth emulating.

The Call Together

I believe the leaders of these 12 churches, along with their congregations, represent the only possibility for healing our nation. If only these churches could be multiplied and others like them brought into existence! I believe that is the only real hope providing the only real possibility for healing in this great nation.

You see, I have lived my whole life with this sense of opportunity, a sense of seizing the moment right now to do all we can do in a given time. The second coming of Christ is our biblical mandate to be working creatively and diligently for the sake of His kingdom. As Matthew 24:14 says, "And this gospel of the kingdom will be preached in all the world as a witness to all the nations, and then the end will come" (NKJV).

And so I feel a great sense of urgency for God's Church to respond to the felt needs of our culture with the good news of Christ's redeeming love. It is my prayer that God's people everywhere would use the stories of these churches and apply the principles from them as they seek to make an eternal difference in their own unique communities. As we work together, we will see our urban neighborhoods transformed with the love of Jesus Christ.

But we can no longer sit back and watch the few who are willing.

Why? Because there is a balm in Gilead. There *is* a physician for our land. His name is Jesus Christ. Won't you work with us to bring the healing ointment of His love to our hurting neighbors in America's cities?

If you would like more information about CCDA
or *Urban Family* magazine, please write to:
Christian Community Development Association,
3877 W. Ogden Ave., Chicago, IL 60623,
or call 312-762-0994;
and
Urban Family,
P.O. Box 32, Jackson, MS 39205,
or call 601-354-1563.
For information about the John Perkins Foundation
for Reconciliation and Development, write to:
1581 Navarro Ave., Pasadena,
CA 91103, or call 818-791-7439.